ANDY PRIAULX

ANDY PRIAULX

TRIPLE WORLD CHAMPION

THE AUTOBIOGRAPHY

HarperSport
An Imprint of HarperCollins*Publishers*

First published in 2008 by
HarperSport
an imprint of HarperCollins
London

© Andy Priaulx 2008

1

A CIP catalogue record for this book is
available from the British Library

ISBN 13 978-0-00-728117-6
ISBN 10 0-00-728117-X

Printed and bound in Great Britain by
Clays Ltd, St Ives plc

The HarperCollins website address is
www.harpercollins.co.uk

Mixed Sources
Product group from well-managed
forests and other controlled sources
www.fsc.org   Cert no. SW-COC-1806
© 1996 Forest Stewardship Council
FSC

All photographs supplied courtesy of Andy Priaulx with the
exception of: George Symons: 3 (middle); Guernsey Press: 2 (middle);
Manx Photos: (hillclimb car/endpaper); Rick Gomes: 7 (bottom);
Sutton: 8 (all), 9, 10 (all), 11 (all), 12 (all), 13 (all), 14 (all), 15 (top), 16.

To Jo, Seb, Dannii and family.

CONTENTS

ACKNOWLEDGEMENTS

JO, MY DARLING WIFE, MY ROCK, MY EVERYTHING, this has almost been a re-run of everything we have been through together. Without you, none of this would have been possible.

Thank you for being my biggest fan and having unwavering faith in me. You are the true champion. You have always been there for me when I have been rock bottom and stood by me through my highs and lows. Thank you for believing in my dream and sacrificing a comfortable life; but most of all, thank you for being the best mum in the world.

A special tribute to Mum and Dad for my great upbringing and for being great grandparents. To Dad, for your belief and faith in me, and Mum, thank you for your prayers and for living my dream silently from home.

My little sis, thank you for being so understanding and so supportive, and Ricco for always seeing the positive side of everything I do. Love you, guys.

Louis and Lorna, thanks for being on call 24/7 and for standing in for me and for helping to parent my kids and look after my home.

Tim, what can I say, you have been my foundation, your honesty and loyalty to me and my family will never be forgotten and will never be taken for granted. Nor will your unwavering support, and your investment in my career for absolutely no personal benefit or return. You are family.

Annie B, my circuit mum, has always been there with sage advice and a glass of wine – this lady is the real secret of British motorsport.

My faithful sponsors, without whom I would not have been able to live my dream and express my talents. For your commitment and risk in the early days, I hope you are maximising the benefits now!

My committed and hard working team of technicians and, of course, my race engineer Sam Waes (Sammy), my highly demanding team boss Bart Mampaey and most importantly the long suffering motor racing widows, wives and partners – thank you.

To BMW UK, BMW Belgium and BMW Motorsport, I thank you for your loyalty and for giving me a safe and fast car. Peter Walker, Chris Willows, Jim O'Donnell – many thanks for being so understanding, so supportive and committed. Thanks to Dr Theissen for rewarding my performances and for appreciating my strengths and abilities.

To Jonathan Taylor, for 'making that call' – had he not done so I might not have taken the steps to write this book. The team at HarperCollins have helped me immensely as I negotiated previously unchartered waters.

Timothy Collings, and his son Josh, for their assistance in putting things in order from my ramblings, and Tom Whiting for not losing too much hair waiting for deadlines to come and go. We made it on time in the end!

John Pratt, for vital input on the details surrounding my success and advice along the way in my career. Cheers, Johnny boy.

Kerrie, Lance, Viv and Ash at Juststuf, and Andrew my silent webmaster, a well oiled machine.

To the various people who have jogged my memory – and they are not listed for they know who they are – I hope you are not offended by anything in this book. Although I will worry forever now that I might have offended some-one along the way …

ANDY PRIAULX
Guernsey, June 2008

FOREWORD

by Dr Mario Theissen, BMW Motorsport Director

WHEN I WAS TOLD BY BMW GB that they wanted to sign Andy Priaulx for their assault on the European Touring Car Championship I must admit I had not heard a great deal about him. I was soon to learn about his challenges to get recognised in the motorsport world and how he would go on to be a great ambassador for motorsport and BMW.

Having brought home four titles for BMW his success for the Team has been well recognised, and in securing matching manufacturer's titles we too have proven our status in the competitive world of touring car racing.

What this book spells out is the unrelenting resolve of Andy to achieve the very best results from not only himself but his team and those around him, ensuring that everyone is working to the aim of winning.

Andy has had a fantastic grounding in finding his own sponsorship to survive and pursuing self-taught disciplines to gain impressive results. These qualities allow him to pass his experiences on to our young drivers in Formula BMW, where he has been a chief instructor, and also to the many around the paddock to whom he is always giving encouragement.

After visiting his home in Guernsey on holiday and thoroughly enjoying the experience, it was even more evident to me the work that Andy has put into motor racing. He has come from an island with no race circuit but a great grassroots motorsport heritage; his raw talent developed on the Val des Terres hillclimb amongst granite walls and unforgiving barriers has flourished on the international stage as Andy has risen to become World Champion.

Andy has had to work hard and sacrificed almost everything to achieve his goal. However, he has maintained a personable and totally approachable demeanour and continues to be a terrific mentor for the young drivers of the future, backed totally by his family and a loyal group of friends. His story opens your eyes to how dreams can be achieved.

INTO THE UNKNOWN

'I was just a lad from Guernsey, in an old car, who was driving up the road chasing a dream'

WE ALL WEPT. THE OTHERS MIGHT NOT ADMIT SO NOW, but they did. And it was all my fault. I was leaving home and honestly didn't have a clue where I was going or what I was going to do. I wanted to get away from Guernsey and make something of myself. I was aiming for Silverstone. I was determined to get to Formula One. I wanted to be a professional racing driver. And I believed I could be …

Looking back now, I realise I was so young and inexperienced. I was still just a kid. I had this big idea in my head and I was intent on making it happen. At least I was being true to type. I am a Guernsey man, a stubborn so-and-so, and I was simply behaving as we all do on my home island – in part, acting like a mule.

My dad Graham, mum Judy and sister Fiona, all the family, my friends and my beautiful fiancée Jo … they were standing there in the harbour, and watched and waved as the boat pulled away. The tears flowed a bit. They knew what I wanted and how much I had sacrificed. I think they understood. I was heading off to chase my dream, leaving everyone behind and hoping for the best.

Who could tell what the future held. Did I have the speed? The character? The talent? The raw ability that everyone needs to succeed in motor racing? One thing I certainly did not have was the money. I had a little profit from some used car sales – not much, although probably just enough to live on for a couple of months. But, more importantly, I had my dream and my self-belief.

The sea rolled and the old Commodore ferryboat carried us out into the English Channel. I felt churned up inside but excited and feeling all manner of conflicting emotions: I wanted to stay with everyone ... yet I wanted to go. Although I had previously been away at weekends racing, I'd usually had my family with me, and I had certainly never before been in a situation like this, going to live in another country on my own.

But I was fired by ambition and determined to give it my best shot. Reaching the top for me in those days meant Formula One because I had watched it on television. And if I could not make it to Grand Prix racing, I would still climb as near to the racing summit as I could.

I had my old Volvo estate with me on the ferry and a Hobby caravan, both of which I had bought to live in during the next chapter of my life. And that was it. I would sleep in the caravan – bought cheap on the mainland – and live that way until I could find my feet. That was the plan …

I looked back to the shore. I could see the faces and expressions. Then I could just about make out the shapes and outlines of each one. And then those shapes blurred until all I could see was the Guernsey shoreline. Gradually, the island began to recede from sight and the open sea took over. I tightened my jaw.

As I stood there, on the slow boat crossing over to the English mainland, I thought of the many Guernsey refugees who had fled before the Germans occupied our island during the Second World War. Then it was old folk, children and families fleeing the German soldiers. I am no great historian but I love my home island and I knew England had always been our 'safe refuge', a place to grow up and seek opportunities. So, like many before me, I was following a long-established Guernsey tradition. I was seeking my fortune across the sea.

I had always been a big motorsport fan as had most of my family. But none of us had attempted this before. And, contrary to a lot of ill-conceived rumours and tittle-tattle,

I was not remotely wealthy. My family was just an ordinary, hard-working, Guernsey clan; indeed, the Priaulx name can be traced back in the history books to the far-off days of William the Conqueror. My mum worked, played the piano and was involved with the church. My dad ran a garage, the family business. He was a real hard-working guy. My granddad, Skip, did the same. And they were both racers. They enjoyed life and did well, but neither was born with a silver spoon in sight. And nor was I.

My granddad raced up and down the beaches in the old days – they used to call it sand racing – tearing around out there when the tide was out. He had a yellow car known as 'the flying banana' and as we grew up we loved to hear all the stories. My dad was a fast driver, too – a winner and record-breaker on the hillclimbs. When I was a kid I helped him prepare his cars, dressing up in a set of red racing overalls to do the polishing and spannerwork.

I suppose, because of all that, motorsport was in my blood. I loved skateboards, bikes, karts, motorbikes and anything that moved fast really. I took part in motocross, and went out boating. I grew up outdoors, climbing, running, playing sport and racing around on anything I could lay my hands on. I had a few scrapes, but nothing put me off climbing back on board whatever the vehicle was to have another go. My mum, admittedly, was not always best pleased about that!

I always remember discovering Formula One and getting hooked on it. I recall watching Gilles Villeneuve with my dad and thinking that I'd love to be doing something like that. I don't think, if I am honest, that I have ever held any ambitions outside of motor racing. I just wanted to race. I loved anything with an engine and a throttle: a motorbike, a car, a powerboat – such machines were a real temptation to me. My gut feeling, as I grew up, was that it was fun and I just wanted to play a bit. But as I started to think more about my future, I realised that maybe I had a bit of talent. I wanted to maximise that and so I had a real burning desire to push myself forwards.

As the boat chugged on, I reflected on all these things. My granddad was a big influence as, too, was my dad. But I think the one thing that drove me to grab my chance to leave Guernsey and seek my fortune came when I saw my granddad lying sick in hospital. At the time I was working for my father at the garage as a sort of car-valet man, salesman, mechanic and general dogsbody. I was doing whatever it took to make money and keep things going. Like all the Priaulx clan I was, and have always been, a very hard-working fellow.

I remembered that my granddad looked so ill and I thought if ever I found myself in that situation I would want to have lived my life to the maximum. I think that was the spark for me, and the really strong feeling to leave the island came there and then. In that way, my granddad was my inspiration. He supported me, and my racing, and he loved it. I had been away to France, to a racing school at Magny-Cours just a while before, so I was really motivated and keen.

A friend of mine, Bill Bristow, had found the caravan for us. I say 'us' because Jo, my then fiancée, and me had planned everything: I would go to England first and get established and she would follow later. Jo and I have always been a team and make all our decisions together. She would stay and work to try and build up as much of a financial reserve as she could and then join me. We had no idea how it would work out.

We decided on the caravan because it made sense. We did not have much cash to throw around and I had no job waiting for me. The caravan was 15 years old and I paid something like £1,500 for it.

My dad was very supportive, always 100 per cent behind me. He thought it was the right move to go to the United Kingdom to learn all about circuit racing. He knew I had the speed – from my hillclimb career – and felt the best place to learn would be at a race circuit, or as close as I could get to one. Well, living inside Silverstone in a caravan would be just the ticket! I'd had a bit of a special memory of Silverstone, too, from watching the British

Grand Prix in 1987 when Nigel Mansell won following a titanic tussle with Nelson Piquet, his Williams team-mate. He had also won at Brands Hatch in 1986, again after a big battle with Piquet, and because of his determination he has always been one of my heroes.

I also knew Jo would support me, of course. She and dad would always be there on the end of the phone when I needed them. My dad always told me that the Priaulxs were risk-takers – people who wanted to push the boat out as far as possible. My granddad was just the same. He took big risks in business in Guernsey, such as acquiring the Fiat agency in the fifties, and succeeded. So I had to get it together. That meant being in the right place at the right time. I knew it would be no easy challenge.

As I sat on the boat looking back and thinking ahead, I knew that had I stayed in Guernsey I would always have been known as 'Andy Priaulx – Graham Priaulx's son'. And I did not want that. My dad was well known for his garage, his work and his racing – he had quite a reputation on the island. But I wanted to be myself, not just another Priaulx.

I knew that when I left Guernsey I would be leaving everything behind me. I would be starting a new life, yet I still felt very sad. I had all the doubts I expected to have, about leaving the family and the family business. My dad had taught me a lot. I knew how to sell, present myself and set up deals.

Take the caravan, for example. You are not really allowed to have a caravan in Guernsey so I had to be careful how I brought it in and used it. Obviously, I was not using it for tourism! I was going the other way. I cleaned and serviced it, made sure the gas worked and hooked it up. I then filled it with supplies and connected it to the Volvo. And my ticket? I had negotiated a deal with the boat company to travel for free, but I had to go on the slow boat that took six or seven hours to make the crossing. But that was just typical of how I did things then. I liked making deals, being decisive and trying to make things happen.

I realised, too, that it was probably a relief for my family, and my dad in particular, to know I had made the decision to go to England. While working at the garage I was also concentrating on phoning teams and finding sponsorship for my racing career. To be honest, the wages I was asking my dad for were too high. I knew that much.

My mum did not really feature in the decision-making at all. She was just happy doing her church work and playing her music, and making sure there was dinner on the table. She did not want to be involved that much. But I knew she would miss me as I would her. We had always been close. And, of course, there was Jo. My life had changed after meeting her. I just felt sure, with Jo, I could achieve my dreams.

* * *

There was no welcome party and no tears when I arrived in England. As I drove off the ferry at Portsmouth I was excited at the prospect of the adventure that lay ahead, even though I had no idea how it would turn out. There I was, in the old Volvo, pulling the old caravan, and heading north away from the coast. It was a bit of a heart-tugging moment. I was hardly driving a fast car and looked like anything but a racing driver as I drove towards Silverstone. And I did not know, after Jo had sold the little house we had bought in Guernsey, how much we would struggle desperately for money and find it difficult to survive at times.

I feared it might be difficult, but I was confident that I had it in me to succeed. I had to make it work. I had to believe in my talent, secure deals, get sponsors and build my career. There were debts from the previous year but – little did I know then – there were to be much bigger and more daunting financial worries ahead of me as I struggled to find my way up the motor racing ladder. People would perhaps laugh at me, but I was determined to prove myself, just as I had done at school when I was the victim of bullying. Then I had to learn to defend myself and survive. This was going to require the same mindset, but quite different skills.

I knew I had a lot to learn and a lot to prove. I had taken such a big risk but I had convinced myself it was a calculated gamble. After all, how many young men of my age – I was then only 23 – would leave a place as isolated and remote as Guernsey to live in a caravan on another island without a confirmed job or any source of income? And all because I reckoned I had enough speed and skill as a racing driver to make it. Looking back, I am not sure I would have done it if I knew then what I know now.

And I was a Guernsey lad. That meant I was used to living in a place where everyone, in general, trusted one another and where we never really locked up our homes; we always left doors and windows open because we knew it was relatively safe. It was the same with cars and car windows. You just did not believe, let alone expect, that anyone would ever think of stealing from you, your home or your car. Crime like that was so rare as to be exceptional in Guernsey.

It was very different as I drove up the A34 looking for somewhere to rest, eat and stretch my legs. It was busy, crowded, and just not as easy-going. I was wet behind the ears all right. I was new to all this, and had to adjust and learn a few things fast. Living in England was going to be very different from staying in Guernsey. The people were different. The way of life was different. And attitudes were very different. It was not as friendly and certainly nothing like as laid-back as I had been used to.

I was just a lad from Guernsey, in an old car, who was driving up the road chasing a dream. Had it not been for my family and some very important friends who had backed me, however, I would not have even been there. Like any other aspiring racing driver, I owed a lot of people a lot of favours and, in many cases, quite a lot of money. But, like me, they believed in my talent – or at least they believed I had enough to stand a chance of making the big time and repaying my debts.

I have always been someone inspired by facing adversity. That is when I am at my strongest. I dig deep, and can find inner strengths to fight back and win. I was not one of the biggest of kids, but I was pretty wiry and tough, and have always been strong for my size. I am tough mentally, too. That's another byproduct of being bullied at school and learning to look after myself. I don't let things defeat me in advance – instead I will work out my own way of winning, making sure I know what I am going to do. I can visualise things and use that technique to help me succeed.

Back then, though, as I drove up through the English counties, I could not even visualise where I was going to park the caravan that first night. Or if it would be safe. Or how I would get to sleep. Did I know how to park up easily and legally? Did I have enough food? How was I going to get started on the job? The motor racing season was about to start. I had some contacts and plenty of ideas but nothing in this business is definite … I knew that. Yet I had so much enthusiasm, belief and desire that I knew I would get there somehow, one way or another. If I am honest, I don't think I even cared how I would do it. I just *knew* I would succeed, whatever it took ...

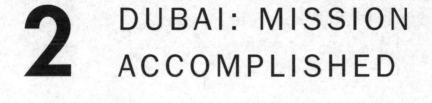

2 DUBAI: MISSION
ACCOMPLISHED

'As the applause went up all around me,
I thought back to when I first went to England,
alone and penniless, but hungry
for success. It seemed
like an age ago …'

SEVEN YEARS AND A FEW MONTHS LATER, I went to Heathrow and I boarded a plane to Dubai. For me, it was another flight to meet my destiny. So much had happened in my life, since that drive from home to Silverstone and I felt everything was finally coming together for me. It was *my* time. Mind you, not many other people felt or thought that way. I was 12 points behind Dirk Muller at the top of the European Touring Car Championship and, as far as I could tell, I was the only man in the world who knew I was on the brink of winning my first international motor racing championship with BMW Team GB. It was my secret. I had prepared for it. I was dreaming of it. I had locked my mind on to that ambition. I just knew it was going to be me who took that title.

In those intervening years, I had answered a lot of my own questions. I had proved to myself, and a lot of other people, that I was a fast and potentially excellent racing driver. I had grown up, too. I was married. I was a family man with two children. We were back in Guernsey, living on the island. Life had given me some encouraging signs and I had survived a few warning shots that reminded me of the fragility of it all. Jo, now my wife, had been very ill when she gave birth to our second child Danniella in November 2003. Little Dannii was five weeks premature when she arrived at The Princess Elizabeth Hospital in Guernsey. I was absent. I was away again, chasing my dream of the moment, on the other side of the world in Macau. Like her older brother Seb, she had a fight on her hands, but she came through. She was a fighter and a survivor: a true Priaulx ...

All these thoughts drifted through my mind as I flew across Europe and down to the Persian Gulf. Blue skies, clear cloudless atmosphere and dry land masses passed below – and then the shimmering blue sea. It was not green, not like Guernsey. But it was a water-lapped coast-line with sunshine – and, yes, there were a few boats! – and it was evocative of my home. I liked what I saw as I looked out of the window. On that plane, out to Dubai, I remember thinking to myself that I deserved to be champion – and whether I won it or not, I was going to prove to everybody that I was the best driver out there that week-end. This was going to be the conclusion of my extended *rite de passage*.

I had found out, on my journey to Dubai, that the Schnitzer team, the BMW outfit with a fantastic record of 30 years of great success in motor racing, had been there the previous week, driving in the race 'taxi car' (a race car tuned up to be used for giving passenger rides). As a driver in with a mathematical chance to win the championship, and as a BMW driver who was therefore part of 'the family', doing the taxi rides for the sponsors gave us vital experience of a circuit I had never seen before, albeit from the data and, perhaps just as important, the demands of a climate with high temperatures, colossal heat and heavy humidity.

This kind of thing – the taxi-rides for sponsors and guests – is something that goes on quite a lot, particularly at new events and circuits. In this case, it was a brand new circuit. Nobody had ever been there before. So, any laps you can get in are a great advantage. I knew it was going to be a great struggle to match BMW Team Germany – who are always the team to beat in the series – and prove that I was the best driver that season. Then I found out that these guys had been in Dubai for two days of testing! It was an advantage – one which I missed – which meant they had their own extra special bit of preparation. Such is the experience of the other teams.

It just goes to show how competitive the European Touring Car series actually is at the very top level. The name of that team, AC Schnitzer, had for years been synonymous with great motor racing and great successes with BMW. I think the combination of the excellent BMW automotive engineering with the motor sports development work of Herbert Schnitzer and his boys made the Schnitzer racing team one of the most successful and well-known touring car teams in the history of motor sports.

And, there we were – the considerably less-well-resourced Team GB outfit, run by Bart Mampaey's Racing Bart Mampaey (RBM Team) based in Mechelen, Belgium – trying to maintain our David v Goliath scenario and lift the title. The RBM Team is run brilliantly by Bart and his, and their, record of triumphs against far more experienced and 'bigger' rivals has given him a reputation that he thoroughly deserves. In many respects, we were well-suited to one another because we were both unsung contenders who wanted to create success where it was not expected. Bart knew what he was doing, too. His father Julian ran the Racing Team in the 1970s and 1980s and he collected three victories, with BMW, in the famous Spa-Francorchamps 24-Hours race. Bart, of course, was there and learned everything he could about running a racing team before he went on to do it himself. So, he was a guy steeped in racing and he was also just as meticulous in his preparations as I am – no wonder we worked so well together!

In the context of the race in Dubai, there was no doubting that we faced a major if not massive challenge if we were to find the perfection we needed to beat the others. But I was not too worried. I had done my own extra special bit of preparation, too, and I was fitter, sharper and more ready for it than I had ever been.

When we rolled our car out at the circuit, I had to learn the track from scratch. So, I went about crawling on my hands and knees and I learned every bump, every little bit of camber and every little bit of kerb at that place. My friend Chris Cramer even taught me to climb trees and look at the track in a very different way, which provided another edge. Maybe the extra help that I thought had been given to the Schnitzer team worked to my advantage. I was motivated and I was so fit. It was just one extra reason to overcome the odds. I worked with my team on every detail we could think of to improve our performance and in the end we ended up with the best car we had ever rolled out up until that point. I felt confident, but I was racing into the unknown.

Before the races, I said to my engineer Sam Waes: 'I don't know about you Sam but this feels like a Hockenheim-type circuit to me ...' And I remember my car was really good at Hockenheim. Sam said to me: 'Yeah, I have the same feeling.' It was good that we were thinking on the same wavelength then. It gave us both a sense of extra confidence.

In the first free practice session, my car was just sensational. I looked at the others and I saw they were really struggling. The competitor in me said: 'Yeah, you have come here and tried to outdo me, but we have come with the better car or, if not, at least the better package ...' We knew we were right on the pace and I felt I was right on the money.

Then, in qualifying, I put it on pole by more than a second! It was incredible. the competition were absolutely nowhere by comparison. They were struggling badly and I was the man in charge. They were gutted. The other drivers had produced nothing. And there was little old me, the guy from Guernsey with the almost unpronounceable name, on pole position. It was a triumph for the small team, too. We were all racing for BMW, whether it be for the GB Team, as in my case, or those representing Italy, Spain and Germany, but there was plenty of healthy and competitive rivalry. I think we all fed on that. I certainly did. That night Jo and I went back to my very luxurious hotel and had a nice meal. It was a great evening. I knew what was happening and I felt I was in control all the way.

The pressure must have eaten into and wrecked Dirk Muller's brain because he had a terrible weekend whereas

I drove two good races. Alfa were really, really fast in Dubai, so Gabriele Tarquini beat me twice, but I knew that I only needed to finish second or higher, to win the championship in race two. It was always going to be tight at the end. I expected it to be that way. However, I must admit that it worked out tighter than anyone could have foreseen.

I was leading the first race for a while but there was an Alfa in my mirrors, getting faster and faster and faster. It was Tarquini. I just managed to hold him off until the very end, when he slipped past me and I finished second. I think it was enough, at that point, to rule Alfa Romeo out of the running for the championship. Dirk had struggled and I had closed the gap, but he was still ahead of me.

We started race two with the reverse grid. That meant I was down in seventh place. I think Dirk finished the first race outside the top ten, so I was ahead of him on the grid again. When the race started, there was a big accident at the fourth corner – and I was involved in it. Jan Magnussen rolled, Alex Zanardi tried to avoid him and in doing so he clouted me. The impact damaged my right rear suspension and I thought that was it. Race over. Championship over. Dream over. Oh, my God. I just could not believe it. My heart sank.

It was so sudden. And there I was, crawling back to the pits, almost sideways, with the car wobbling all over the place. From that early high, I was now feeling despondent. But the next thing, the team came over the radio and said: 'Andy. Andy. Do not come into the pit lane. The race is red-flagged. Do not come into the pit lane.' More great strategy from Bart. It was red-flagged because Magnussen was on his head – so I had a chance again. The red flag meant the original race was stopped and aborted. A new race, with a new start, would follow.

So I pulled onto the grid and the team managed to fix my car. I remember someone took a few photographs of the scene. There was a picture of myself, and Dirk, sitting against the pit wall helpless while our mechanics buzzed around in the heat with parts and tank tape. He looked really nervous and I looked cool but under pressure.

When the race re-started, I made a brilliant start, cut through the field and managed to climb up to third place. Then, I pulled a great move up the inside of Jörg Muller and was up into second. Tarquini was ahead of me and behind me was James Thompson who was faster than me. I was under massive pressure. That was where my fitness really came in because on every single corner on every single lap I had to defend. I had to hold Thommo off for the whole race in temperatures of 70 degrees Celsius. It was absolutely, stunningly, extraordinarily and crazily baking hot inside my car. If I had given up my position I would have given up the championship and I had no intention of doing that. Dirk was stumbling around in sixth or seventh position but still fighting through the field. I knew I could not afford any slips. The pressure was huge, monstrous and incessant. Combined with the heat, it was a tortuous race for everyone.

I was behind Dirk in the points and I could not let it go. I would not let it go. I fought like a madman to defend from Thommo. Dirk was having all sorts of scraps behind me but I hung on. I finished second. We had to wait for Dirk to come through before we knew if I had won the championship. It seemed like an eternity.

Then, finally, as I cruised around in my oven of a car with my sweat-soaked race suit undone a little to find some cool air, I got the call. It came literally just after the finish line on my slow-down lap. I was waiting, waiting and waiting and then the call came: 'Andy, you have done it … You are the champion!'

I could hardly believe it. I was the European Touring Car Champion. I had won my first international motor racing title. It was an amazing moment. I could hardly take it in.

Jo and I had survived and climbed our mountain. I thought of my dad, my mum, my sister and my granddad, how proud my family would feel. I thought of my kids and all the people who had believed in me and worked to help me.

The teams were out in the pit lane when I came in. They all lined up and clapped me in – an absolute honour. My mum and dad were there in tears. My dad had Parkinson's and he was shaking a lot from the nerves of the whole thing but he was so happy for me. Jo was there too. I stood on the car and jumped off the roof. It was amazing. I had such a lump in my throat, it was unbelievable. As I stood there, it felt like a dream.

There were some tears. But this time, they were tears of joy. We had achieved it. We had won. I knew things would change for Jo and I. It was not the end; it was the start. No wonder we all wept again ... At last, after the caravan, the hard times and our struggle to survive, we had arrived. That afternoon, in the heat of Dubai, standing on that podium with my family there to share our joy, I knew I had realised my dream. But I knew, too, that it was just the first step.

I took that championship, in the end, on number of races won. Dirk Muller and I finished level on 111 points for the season. It was that close, so close. My superior preparation, that of the team and my absolute determination to succeed had carried me through. That is the way I saw it. I knew I would win and that in my mind nobody else had a chance.

After that final race, Frank Diefenbacher, one of the Seat team drivers, drove his car back to *parc ferme* and fell out of it. He collapsed with heat exhaustion. He was taken away and put on a drip. The poor guy was so knackered he could hardly stand up, barely breathe and had no chance of speaking properly for a while. He was utterly crushed by those conditions.

Yet he had been just one place in front of Dirk at the finish of the race.

As I let things sink in, I realised that if he had flaked out a lap earlier, or before that, I would not have been champion. Dirk would have passed him and my dream would have been all over. But his courage in producing that fighting finish and crossing the line had secured my first international title. Those are the margins you work with all the time in motor racing.

Not only did I prove I was the quickest driver there that year, but I won the championship against all the odds – against the might and experience of BMW Schnitzer and N-Techology Alfa Romeo who were doing anything possible to win the championship. I do believe that Schnitzer are one of the best racing teams in the world. They are a top team in every way and I have a lot of respect for them. Their budget must have been double our budget. The Alfa Romeo team with their four cars were also very strong and resourced well, too. They had a great driver lineup:

Gabriele Tarquini, Fabrizio Giovanardi, Augusto Farfus Jr, Thommo … all good drivers.

I thought it was pretty impressive to go into that European series and to win there so quickly – in only my second season. In my first year, they could not even pronounce my name. I remember when I went for an interview with a local television station in Guernsey and they told me they had gone to the first race, in Valencia, and asked a load of the other drivers about me. Every one of them said, 'Well, we sort of know who he is, but we don't know much about him'. My BMW colleague Jörg Muller was interviewed and he said, 'Ja, of course, we know him, and now he is in BMW – but he hasn't proved anything'.

I just shook my head and said to myself: 'You know nothing.' I have always said that my critics have helped me and being the underdog has helped me too. Those things have kept me very hungry. I could have been the racing driver who turns up with the big shades, the glamorous watch and the sun tan and just straps himself into an ultra-fast car and goes out and does the job. That would have been lovely, but it has never been like that for me.

My work ethic has always been to roll my sleeves up and graft. It has had to be. It carries over from my ordinary life and always has done. I have the habit of wanting to do it myself and wanting to see a job done well, even if I have to help. This still spills into my non-racing life too. Not long ago, we had builders doing some work on our house in Guernsey. I got so frustrated that I actually rolled up my sleeves and got stuck in there myself. I really enjoyed it. And I'm sure I did the job pretty well! I learned to work like that early in my life and it has never left me. My family always worked hard and I hope we always do.

There is no doubt that I have needed that kind of grit in my touring car career. Nobody really believed in me to start with and I had to overcome a lot of other people's doubts. But when I won the 2004 European Championship everybody was clapping, all of them, up and down the pit lane. All the big teams were saying 'Bloody hell! He's actually won it. He has gone and done it ...' I remember them all coming out of their garages in Dubai and I was in tears. It was so emotional for me.

In 2003, I had showed my speed and people knew that I was good, but they still did not believe it. They thought Alfa would still be the number one, but my grit would not let me give up. I *never* give up. After 2004, everybody predicted that the competition would be back strongly – and they were right because 2005 was tougher, 2006 was even tougher still and 2007 was even tougher than that! But I won all three times, taking the title and keeping it. The problem, for me, has been that with each passing year, more and more people did not want me to win. Not only did they want to see a change, they wanted the power structure to work. If there was going to be someone dominating that series, turning it into a private empire like Michael Schumacher seemingly did in Formula One, they certainly did not want it to be me.

Unlike Formula One, Touring Cars is a contact sport and the politics are such that when things go in a certain kind of way you can end up being barged off the track. Yes, literally. There is also the penalty known as success ballast, reverse grids and rule changes all the time. The rules are not even necessarily the same for all the teams. At different times there has been one rule for one and something else for the others. I have always sensed that there was a huge amount of respect for me, but also that there has certainly been a big drive to stop me from winning the championship year on year. In a way, I guess it is understandable. But I have taken no notice. I have just gone out there and done my best to do my job. I have ground out the races and the results by squeezing everything I could from the package we had each year.

It was the same grit that has worked for me all through my career. It is the grit I saw in Nigel Mansell and that I have also seen in Lance Armstrong and a few other people. Maybe it is a bit of bloody-mindedness, too. And you do need talent. Do not think it can be done without talent. But talent alone is not enough. Everything you achieve in life needs hard work and there are few, if any, people who break that rule. I have always worked to achieve everything from polishing cars for my dad, selling on the forecourt, hustling to find sponsors and teams and then improving my own racing by looking, listening and learning at every opportunity. I have also worked tremendously hard at my fitness and I am sure that it was one of the decisive factors in 2004.

Before the Dubai decider that year, there was a little bit of time off after the Oschersleben meeting. I was 12 points behind, but I still had not given up. I had decided that I would do anything and everything to compete and stay in contention. After you have made a decision in your life to leave home and pursue your dream, like I did when I left Guernsey, it is not asking much to work your socks off to keep that dream alive.

I trained very hard. And I trained in a way that seemed logical to me, but caused quite a stir later on when a lot of other people found out about it. I put my race suit on, I put my helmet on and I got in the sauna at Kings Club, a gym and fitness place, in Guernsey, two minutes' drive from my house. I was doing boxing in the sauna in full race gear. It was a public club, so plenty of people would have seen me there in my race overalls and helmet, but I did not give a damn what anybody thought. I trained on a bike. I did 'boxercise', sit-ups, press-ups, running … I did everything

I could. I stayed in the sauna for the length of two races, an hour and a half, nearly every day. I just wanted to be quick in Dubai and I would do anything I could to help myself. People said I was crazy and maybe I was, but it worked.

I trained really hard and physically I was fit. I felt super-fit. But, more importantly than that, most importantly of all, I was mentally fit. My head was ready. My mind was clear and set. I did a lot of meditation. I knew that Dubai, in September, would be awful. I knew we were preparing for ambient air temperatures of 42 or 43 degrees Celsius. And I knew it was going to be humid. It would be even hotter in the cars and it would be desperately uncomfortable. Staying calm, clear-headed and sharp, capable of making decisions under extreme stress and pressure was going to be an important part of the weekend's work.

When I got off the plane, I felt sick with the heat. It was so humid that everything steamed up – my sunglasses, the car – everything! I arrived pretty early in the week because the race was on a Friday. I wanted to be ready in every way. I was collected from the airport by a driver and taken in a nice big car to the Mina A' Salam hotel which is absolutely gorgeous.

It smelt beautiful and I could not believe my luck. I had to take a boat to my hotel room. It was a little Abra and I was filled with a kind of excitement, a confident feeling of anticipation mixed with a few nerves. The whole place, the whole experience was just fantastic and I wanted to go out and complete the picture with a great job all weekend.

I woke up in the morning, got out of bed and, there I was, on a beach. I could see the sea. It felt a bit like Guernsey again and I definitely drew something from that. I also had a lovely 7-Series BMW given to me for the weekend and so, for me, the whole experience felt a bit special for the first time. I had gone from living in a caravan to being treated to nice hotels and luxury cars. And, I have to say, it was great!

Dirk may have been leading the championship and I am sure everyone expected him to win, but that takes no account of me. I am such a determined so-and-so. I never give in. And there, in that hotel room, with that car and that view, I felt so much energy. So I enjoyed myself – and I went out and won my first major international title.

We, BMW Team GB, were a one-car team. That in itself was a disadvantage when it came to a lot of the races because we could not do the slip-streaming, by using a team-mate for tow, like others did. But it was not the end of the world. I knew how strong we could be from the year before and I was not intimidated at all by the opposition. We had finished 2003 very strongly and all through 2004 I was convinced I could achieve my goals.

I started the season pretty competitively. I was up there, not dominant by any means because teams had been testing all through the winter – before I had even negotiated my contract – but still pretty sharp. Compared to the previous year when I was learning my way at that level really, I started winning much earlier.

Then, of course, the 'success ballast' came into play. The more successful you were, the more ballast you had to carry in the next race. It was a ploy by the series administration to try and keep the racing close and exciting and in its way it worked. But I never felt it was fair. It just meant that if you did your job and you were the fastest, once you proved it and started winning they tried to make sure you could not win any more!

That was not my only problem though. I remember feeling like I was a marked man that year. And it was only because I was fast and successful. People were already starting to get quite cold with me and I guess it came from the political pressures that were created by massive expectations generated by the big factory teams. Obviously, there was some tension among the teams and the atmosphere was getting a bit harder, a bit more serious; more tense, I suppose. In the first year, everyone was patting me on the back (I ended up as the only BMW driver after race one at the end of the first year in the final race at Monza). Then, after that, the affection seemed to dry up. I was no longer just a driver in the pack, but a threat to some people's self-appointed intentions, in terms of racing success and titles.

There were no more pats on the back. I guess Lewis Hamilton had to go through a similar sort of experience after his brilliant rookie season in Formula One with McLaren Mercedes. When you have proved yourself, everyone else says: 'Ok, now really prove yourself because we are the big boys and we bounce back ...' I do not know how personal it was, but in some ways I was still a bit naïve and less experienced than these guys. I understood the sport, but all the politics was a bit of a new thing for me. So, I did what I knew best – I got on with it, I put my head down and I worked and worked at everything.

I had some good wins that year. I won at Magny-Cours, Hockenheim, Brno, Donington and Oschersleben. The key moment during the season was reaching a point, about three-quarters of the way through, when I was in with a really serious chance of winning the championship. At some stages I was leading, at others I was behind, what with the extra weight and the reverse grids (the finishing order of the top eight drivers was reversed after the first race at each meeting for the second race).

I was always there in the mix. The year before, I had come from way behind and almost stolen the title right at the end, but this time I was one of the main contenders all season. I was loving it and I was pushing hard.

I had earned my position to be there, fighting for the championship, and there was still a really good chance that I could win it. Dirk did his job well but in Oschersleben it did not work out for him. I was quicker than him in qualifying, I made a great start in race one, got ahead of him and made sure I put two cars between us before going on to win. Then in race two, to put it bluntly and honestly, I was driven off the road!

I was crashed into and it seemed like the fairytale story was not going to happen – or was certainly not going to be allowed to happen. I know that, to many observers, it seemed that the other drivers had decided among themselves that the small guy was not going to win the championship.

I was an underdog who had put together a really good season, but I was not what they wanted to be declared as a champion. I felt I had earned my position, but a few drivers decided that it was not what they wanted (maybe for the credibility and prestige of the series) and a few teams had decided that it was not what they wanted either – and it was just sour grapes. It was not just in Oschersleben that this kind of thing happened either.

I was driven off the road in a few places point-blank that season. Maybe it was just one way of giving a newcomer a warm welcome to a series ... However, Dirk gained eight points on me in that second Oschersleben race, leaving him with one hand on the championship, 12 points ahead going into Dubai.

It was all rather difficult for me to understand then. It was, I suppose, just a part-manifestation of the politics that go with a big manufacturer series like that when there is a lot at stake and there are a lot of big name drivers with their reputations on the line. It is not personal at all and I have never once lost my faith in the integrity or the honesty of any competitor, but I do think that it does show there is more to motor racing than often meets the eye.

For example, after I won the title at the end of the season in Dubai, Dr Mario Theissen gave me a present – something that I was delighted to receive. It was a chance to drive the Williams BMW Formula One car. It was something I had always wanted and it proved to me that for all the tension between the racing teams, the BMW people were very appreciative of my efforts and supportive of my career.

That was when I first met Sam Michael and the other Williams guys and they were really nice. I could tell that they had watched my season, but they knew it was just a test for a Touring Car driver, nothing serious. What they did not know is that I had been in the gym since I knew I was testing, working out every day. I was very determined about the test and immediately I showed my speed. So that one chance turned into lots more tests the following year and I am very proud of that. That was a great moment for me to choose to go the touring cars route and then still end up with a little job in Formula One. I achieved another of my own dreams that way, thanks to Dr Theissen and BMW.

But I digress; back to that glorious day in Dubai. After everyone had calmed down a little and the celebrations started to wane I went back to my hotel room and said to Jo: 'Our life is going to change.' I thought at the time that it would change and I would become a big name, a big personality that was well-respected in British sport.

But that just did not happen immediately. It was a bit of a surprise to me because my championship win was such a big story in motor racing and throughout most of Europe, if not the world. It showed me how conservative some sections of our media can be, but since then I have learned to understand it better. But it is still a bit of a shock. I was the first British European Champion since Tom Walkinshaw, 19 years earlier, so I had done something pretty special and I had also won in adversity. I had showed my determination. I remember reading all the e-mails afterwards, some really famous people were writing to me ... Derek Warwick, Walkinshaw, all really nice people and well-known, too. I thought 'Wow this is awesome – my life is going to change!' But it did not, at least not right away.

We all flew back from Dubai together on the Saturday. My sister Fi flew back with us, and my brother in-law

Rick and their son, Jacob, were there too. When we landed at home, we walked through the airport in Guernsey and I can remember hearing a load of noise. I honestly had no idea who it was or what it was about. I walked out and all of my friends and more of my family were waiting. My two kids greeted me – and all the Guernsey fraternity turned out to meet me at the airport, as I walked out.

They were clapping as I walked through and I nearly lost it, I nearly broke down in tears. It was amazing for them to turn out. I felt so much emotion. Channel TV were there, everything. I do not think the Bailiff turned out, but he did the following year when I won the world championship. All the local Sports Council people were there, but also old people, people I had never met before, and they had all got behind me and watched the races. It was an amazing feeling. It meant so much.

Amidst all the fanfare, I could not help but reflect on my journey from that Guernsey boy, who nobody thought could win anything, to a man with a little bit of a success, and then to European champion. It had not been easy. That was for sure. It had been bloody difficult. On several occasions, it had looked like it was never going to happen for me. As the applause went up all around me, I thought back to when I first went to England, alone and penniless, but hungry for success. It seemed like an age ago, but then, in that instant, it all seemed worth it in a way that I could never have imagined. After my Silverstone years, I really felt I had achieved something.

3 HARD TIMES AT SILVERSTONE

'Well, so what, Priaulx? Oh, you won a few hillclimbs, racing against old farmers, eh? Who the hell do you think you are?'

THERE IS AN OLD SAYING IN MOTOR RACING: 'Standing still is like going backwards at 100 mph.' In other words, you have to make progress all the time or you will soon find yourself left behind. It is perpetual motion. Everyone else is trying to go faster the whole time, so the moment you slacken off you will be overtaken. I think you get the idea.

The same kind of thinking dictates that once you have climbed your first mountain, you need to decide which one is next and then go out there and do it again. There is no room for sentiment. And there is no time to take a breather. Jo and I knew that because we had been climbing for years and fighting all the way. So, on the way back from that fantastic first European Touring Car Championship title win in Dubai in 2004, we knew that the next big challenge would be even tougher: we had to be faster, stronger and even better organised if we were to return the following season and 'do it again' – in other words, retain that championship crown.

Being from Guernsey was a big help, of course. We were not about to lose our heads, celebrate too much or lose touch with the earth beneath our feet. We had only to mention that kind of thing and we both knew what it meant. We had been through so much together, over so many years, that we were not going to get this far and then waste it. After all, had it not been for Jo and our respective families, I do not think we would have succeeded.

The Guernsey blood in our veins was a real strength not just then, as we enjoyed success, but all the way through. And it still is. When I left home in 1997 and towed that caravan to Silverstone, it was not just the end of the first part of my life; it was the start of the second. But in both I continued to be true to my Guernsey roots, and am proud of what I've achieved on behalf of my home island.

The day I arrived in Portsmouth and began the journey up the A34 was the beginning of my passage to independence, adult life and my own form of success. I had done well in the British Hillclimb Championship, while living at home and supported by my dad and family, but I had not really done anything in the eyes of the people involved in the single-seater racing heartland of British motor sport. I like to think I had actually 'turned professional' in 1996 – a year earlier – when I visited my granddad, Skip, in hospital after he became ill. I remember thinking then, at his bedside, that I had to do something special with my life. For a year, I tried to do some racing in Formula Renault. I had some sponsors, but not, by a long way, the whole package. My father, Graham, had to guarantee loans and helped me out every way he could. Even though I had stopped working for him at the garage he still let me sell my own cars on the site. Jo's mum and dad were great, too, even loaning me the first £2,000 I needed to buy a car and get started. I was wheeling and dealing, cleaning cars for my dad, trying to hustle up sponsorship and fit in some races to prove I had the speed and talent. I thought that was tough – but nothing like as hard as it turned out to be the following year when I did get to Silverstone. Until then, I did not believe it could have got any worse for me or that I could have been more desperate. I was wrong. Very wrong.

I had made some contacts during the previous year, when I was trying to get myself a drive. One was Mike O'Brien who ran the Speedsport Formula Three team. He was a guy I admired in the same way as I did Nigel Mansell. Both have done it all for themselves, battling up from the bottom when they did not have enough money to go racing, and yet proving just what can be achieved with a never-say-no, never-say-die attitude.

After sleeping one night in a lay-by on the side of the road, somewhere on the journey up to Northamptonshire, I arrived at the Home of British Motor Racing full of hope. After all, I was the reigning British Hillclimb Champion. I may have started my first Formula Renault race at Thruxton at the back of the grid, but I think I had managed to secure a podium finish before the end of the season. I was not a complete novice. I believed in my speed. And I had talent. The only problem was that I was the only one who really knew that.

I had a good feeling about Mike O'Brien. He had managed to sponsor himself so I knew he would be my first port of call at Silverstone. So he had this guy turn up in a Volvo estate with a caravan in tow, and declare: 'I'd really like to go racing!' and 'Where can I park this thing?' and 'Can we do a deal? If I find any sponsorship from the street then I'll put it into your team.'

And, in fairness, Mike replied: 'Yeah, I've got an area behind the back of the workshop.'

So I went round the back and it was, well, a working backyard, covered in oil stains, hardly pristine, various tins and drums thrown about and a few other bits of debris blowing around in the wind on top of the remains of some oil-soaked gravel that had seen better days. I do not know what I had in mind before I left home, in terms of a place to park the caravan and live, but I remember thinking this was something else. It was hardly a leafy, manicured camping and caravan site. But it was available, and it was in the middle of Silverstone. Mike's boys told me I could hook up a cable through their rear toilet window for power and so there I was.

The old yard was called the 'clinker yard' and for pretty obvious reasons: it was where Mike and his lads did all their engine-oil changes. There were containers everywhere. It was pretty scruffy but I knew it was the closest I was going to get to motor racing with a Formula Three team.

Mike helped me out. I would open my door in the morning, go out of my caravan and into the workshop to see these beautifully painted Formula Three cars. They just looked stunning to me. It was an all-new experience. I had never seen anything like it before.

Mike was very kind and I was very grateful for that. We got along well and became friends, me living in the 'clinker yard' and doing all I could to help out, and Mike giving me some tips, guidance and helping me to find sponsorship. I was skint, of course, and I needed some money not just to race but to live. Mike helped me find a job as a driving instructor at Silverstone and later, when she arrived from Guernsey to join me, helped Jo get a job in the Silverstone ticket office that eventually led to her working in the British Racing Drivers' Club admin department. But, for those months before Jo came over, it was just me and me alone trying to get things going – and it was at this time that the nickname 'Pikey Priaulx' started being used around the place. I did not really mind too much, although I worried it might hinder me in the sponsorship market!

I had a few sleepless nights when I first got to Silverstone. Not only was I worried by the huge challenge I faced and the lack of cash, but also the place seemed to be stalked at night by wild animals and birds. It is not until you sleep outdoors, or in a caravan, that you realise how much wildlife there is and how much noise they all make. The worst came, I think, from the foxes. And it was absolutely freezing cold a lot of the time. I just curled up and hoped for the best.

The first night was the most awful. It was really, really cold and I was lying there in my bed, on my own, tight like a ball with my socks and everything else on. The foxes were making those screaming noises – I think it is something to do with mating! – and I had never heard anything like it before in my life. I was petrified. It sounded like somebody was dying or something. It was also the start of the British motor racing season for which I had no money at all. But I knew I had to get over it.

I realised that to reach the next level in my racing career required a huge investment in myself, and a lot of personal commitment. However, I had known that for a while before I had taken that decision. I remember saying to myself: 'How can I expect people to sponsor me if I'm not prepared to take the financial risk myself and put everything on the line?'.

I spoke to Jo, and to her parents, and my dad, who always supported me. I said: 'Listen, I'm going to leave the business and live in England – for the racing season.' And Dad replied: 'Well, how are you going to pay the mortgage on the house if you are not going to be here working? You're going to be living away.'

So I said: 'We can rent the house out and we'll just go in the caravan.' Eventually, the finance figures were so high that we had to sell the house. That's why Jo stayed behind at the beginning, in order to handle all that while I went off to pursue my motor racing career.

Selling the house meant we could pay off all the debts I had built up from the previous year when I was commuting back and forth to the races. I owed money to the Formula Renault team, not least eight grand's worth of accident damage I had picked up rolling the car after suspension failure during testing at Oulton Park. In the end, Jo moved up to Silverstone to be with me but, for a long time, I was on my own. All we had was that caravan, but at least we had sorted out everything else so we could start afresh.

It was a good feeling not to have those debts anymore but, at the same time, I felt bad because I did not even have a drive. I was a racing driver, living in a caravan at Silverstone, but without a team or a car. And that is where Mike really helped me. I started talking to the teams all around Silverstone, looking for a chance, but I was a man with no fixed abode and not much else. No wonder everyone gave me funny looks at times.

I am an easy-going guy, but I do have a sense of purpose. It may have seemed as if I had been driving down the road with no real destination in mind, but it did not feel like that to me. I started telling people my story and making friends. Of course, they all wanted to know who I was and what I was doing. So I told them: the drive from Guernsey, the night in the lay-by, the dreams ... For a long time I was lonely and sad. I was fulfilling my dream, living at Silverstone, but I was not happy. How could I be?

I woke up some days and could hear the sound of Formula One engines testing around Silverstone. 'Wow! This is it. I am here and living my dream.' Then there were other days, when it was pouring with rain, that I looked out of the window of a steamy caravan, condensation everywhere, and I asked myself: 'What am I going to do?'

At least I knew I was heading towards something. Until that time, Guernsey had been my limiting factor because I had been trying to mix motor racing with my life there, when the former demanded 150 per cent of my attention. It would be very different later once I was established in racing and married with a family. Then, Guernsey brought me something in terms of health, happiness and speed. But in those early days it had been a hindrance.

I had no money, had incurred huge expenses getting from and to the island and did not have the contacts and connections that I needed. I simply did not understand at that time what it took to become a professional driver. I had raw talent with a great feeling for a car, but did not understand things like racing lines, or setting up the car for high- or low-speed, or high- or low-grip configurations. It had to be learned, all of it.

Let us say hillclimbing was table tennis, and I was a top table tennis player. I've got great ball control, a great eye for the ball and I hit everything back. Then, one day, some-body gives me a tennis racquet and says: 'Right, go and play at Wimbledon!' Well, I am going to be in trouble. So I reply: 'Hang on a second, I'm just hitting a small ball. This is a bigger ball. And how do you serve and all that?' That's what it was like. I had a good eye for the ball but no under-standing of how, or what it took, to become a professional. I had to learn it all.

It was no wonder, then, that I felt like a bit of an outsider. I was very fortunate. I had spoken a lot with Mike and he gave me some belief and hope that something might happen. Mike had battled to get to Formula Three level and was now managing Darren Manning, who himself was racing in Formula Three. I would watch him and think to myself: 'I can be like that.' My connection with him became stronger, but at first I think he must have just felt sorry for me.

I had been talking to Mike before because, after my initial Formula Renault season the year before, I had been in contact with all the Formula Three teams. Maybe he saw a kindred spirit in me, another guy like him who was prepared to do anything to make things happen.

I recall having a few designer clothes and put them in the caravan cupboard. At least in there they would stay reasonably clean. They were for my meetings with potential sponsors – when I had arranged them. Every day I got up, washed, shaved, splashed on some aftershave and started work. I hooked up my computer to the power; obviously, I had no access to e-mails and the internet but I could write letters on the computer and make telephone calls. I just got on with it. So, from nine in the morning I sat at the front of my caravan, working at a desk – which was actually a bed – writing, making notes and planning how it was going to happen.

The glow of self-confidence I enjoyed from being crowned British Hillclimb Champion seemed to last for about five minutes. It should have been a glorious step in my career. But that is not what happened. I realised it soon enough, of course, and 1996, 1997 and 1998 were real back-down-to-earth years. I soon found out that hillclimb success meant next to nothing in circuit-racing circles – although I did receive an offer from Paul Stewart Racing to join them in 1995, but turned it down for financial reasons. I soon realised that I was an absolute nobody when it came to proper professional racing in mainland Britain. The attitude was 'Well, so what, Priaulx? Oh, you won a few hillclimbs, racing against old farmers, eh? Who the hell do you think you are?'

I knew I had to build myself a reputation all over again and the only way to do that would to be to win races and grab podiums every week. In that respect, 1996 had been a complete failure and had not given me any platform for the following year when I left home. In that first year, I had been trying to make a name for myself but, in truth, even getting a drive proved difficult. I did a few races, thanks to people like Mike Knight, of the Winfield Racing School at Magny-Cours in France; Tico Martini; Andrew Green, a private sponsor of mine from Jersey; and Masters International, in Formula Renault with Martello Racing – but it was tough going.

I started at the back of the grid at Thruxton and knew there was only one way I could go from there. True enough, I did get better, but it was a very slow process. There were accidents, bills and rising costs. Then Jim Gillespie, the manager of The Mallard hotel in Guernsey, began to help and we borrowed money for the second half of the season when I switched to Startline Racing. That was when my father stepped in as well. My team-mate was Malaysian driver Alex Yoong, who later raced in Formula One. He drove the new car while I had the older model. But it was not long before Jim lost interest and I was left to make the payments on my own. It was very tough but I managed to run in the Formula Renault winter series and produce my first strong finish in a championship before all the money ran out. It was then myself and Mike O'Brien had our first talks about possible Formula Three deals.

I had dreamt about all this but I hardly did anything to prove I might be the next Nigel Mansell. I had tried to reach Formula Three, thinking I was ready for that next step. I had been handling Formula One engines in hill-climbing so I figured I should be able to drive Grand Prix cars on circuits. That was the mentality I had. Looking back, it did not matter one jot because I did not have the money to make it work. In hindsight, what I should have done was win the British Hillclimb Championship with ex-

Formula One engines and then start at the very bottom of the circuit-racing ladder in Formula Ford. That way I could have progressed steadily, and built up both a reputation and those all-important sponsors.

It is easy to see now what I should have done now but at that time it was not so clear. So, in 1997, I tried to do some B-class Formula Three races. It was not a successful venture, however. I ran out of money, found some sponsors, paid for a few races ... and ended up being nowhere. It was tough. I was learning everything the hard way.

That said, one positive thing did come out of the year. I built up some good friendships and, through one, I had a race with Speedsport at Silverstone. Mike O'Brien gave me the chance and, as luck would have it, it was held on the full Grand Prix circuit.

It was not the British Grand Prix support event, but it was still a decent race. I qualified nowhere and looked doomed to struggle again. But fortune smiled on me when it rained heavily throughout the race. I just got that car moving and cut right through the pack.

In fact, I think I might still hold the Speedsport Formula Three record for the most positions made up in a single race. From almost last on the grid I finished tenth. It was quite a large grid with some big players including Formula One-quality guys like Mark Webber, Enrique Bernoldi, Nicolas Minassian and Darren Manning. And I was able to catch these guys because it was wet and I was sliding the car around. I outbraked Guy Smith to take one position. At that time he was winning races and had a reputation far superior to mine, but there he was disappearing behind me.

In the rain, it's less about what car you are in and what you know about driving, and much more about raw instinct. And I had plenty of that. The result made me think I might just be getting somewhere again. The whole team was very pleased. Mike was happy for me but did not want to seem too impressed because that would have meant my not having to provide as much sponsorship money for the team the following year!

At the end of the year, I became involved with TOMS Toyota in Formula Three. Basically, they were looking for somebody to pay for a drive – that was all. They did not come to me because I was good – they did so because I sounded like I was desperate and they needed money. So my dad borrowed some funds, I found some sponsors, other people chipped in and I managed to buy two races.

I was thrilled, but – what a surprise – things did not work out. The car had too much downforce and I was just doing the odd race. I was competing against people who had been in the car all year so I didn't really stand a chance.

By now, aged 24, I was engaged to Jo and we were look-ing forward to a Christmas wedding. I was delighted about that, but my so-called professional life was nothing like as happy as my personal one. The races with TOMS had gone 'pear-shaped' and the accompanying tests had not fared well either. I really needed to impress in my last test with TOMS following the final race of the season. So I hired a driver coach, a guy called John Pratt. It was the best thing I could have done.

The two-day test at Croft in November, ahead of the classic end-of-season Macau race, was for all the top Formula Three runners from the British Championship. It would give me a real benchmark of where I stood. I needed some straightforward unbiased feedback, an honest opin-ion and some good advice. John was great for me. He pointed out some basic errors in my circuit driving tech-nique all due to a lack of experience – and helped me fix them. The next thing I knew I was going faster and faster. I rediscovered my speed. My lap times were good, certainly comparable with the leading pack of British Formula Three drivers and my confidence was restored. The decision to hire John and attend the test had been vindicated. It was a good day and almost deserved a celebration. The only other good news we had around that time came when Jo got promoted from the ticket office to BRDC race admin thanks to Mike O'Brien. It paid the grand rate of £4 an hour!

The boost I gained from that test gave me the lift that, after months of living in the caravan, I badly needed. But I knew it would not signal the end of my problems. Jo and I were planning our wedding, but we still did not have any money. Around Silverstone I was still 'Pikey Priaulx' and would stay like that until I moved out. I felt as if I could compete at a high standard but just didn't have the money to go any further. So, unless something dramatic happened, I could see it would be difficult to start the 1998 season as we packed up our life at Silverstone and went home. However, we left all those worries behind us briefly once we were back in Guernsey where Jo and I were married on 27 December 1997 at St Martin's Parish Church, with our families all around us.

4 A GUERNSEYMAN FOREVER

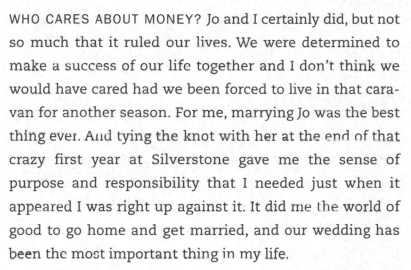

'Fear is something you have to live with but something you learn to ignore.
I tell myself that f-e-a-r stands for "false evidence appearing real"'

WHO CARES ABOUT MONEY? Jo and I certainly did, but not so much that it ruled our lives. We were determined to make a success of our life together and I don't think we would have cared had we been forced to live in that caravan for another season. For me, marrying Jo was the best thing ever. And tying the knot with her at the end of that crazy first year at Silverstone gave me the sense of purpose and responsibility that I needed just when it appeared I was right up against it. It did me the world of good to go home and get married, and our wedding has been the most important thing in my life.

It was a big signal, too. It grounded me and confirmed that with Jo I was now all set for the future I wanted and that, together, we could climb any mountain. Racingwise I knew it would be a battle, but I was confident and still believed in myself. And, importantly, both of our families believed in me.

My Guernsey roots have always been a source of pride to me. I love the place, its way of life, its unique, independent island history and the myriad idiosyncrasies that set it apart not just from Jersey – a place we refer to as 'the other island' – but everywhere else. My family name is entwined with the history of the island and there are many references to the Priaulx name in and around Guernsey – such as the library and one of the football leagues, to mention just two. But we are not the only family with a special association with Guernsey and I am not the only guy to have left the island and achieved success. Nor am I the first person living on the island to write a book.

The island has produced countless people who have done well in many different walks of life. These include the Dotrice family – Roy and his daughters, Michele and Karen – who all became well-known actors; Gerald Edwards, who was the author of the highly-rated novel *The Book of Ebenezer Le Page*; Matthew Le Tissier, who played football for Southampton and England; and many more. Oliver Reed, the famous actor, lived in Guernsey for many years as did John Le Mesurier of *Dad's Army* fame. And Guernsey has supplied the BBC with several presenters, including Dawn Porter and Sarah Montague.

Clearly Guernsey is a place where people with talent can flourish.

It is a place with history, too. Of course, we are part of Britain, being a British Crown dependency, but we have our own anthem, coat of arms and flag along with our own recognised regional language. Guernsey has its own quirks, too. For example, our head of state is, for historic reasons, always known as the Duke of Normandy – in other words, Queen Elizabeth II. And it has been that our head of state is the British monarch since 1204.

Before that the French – the Normans – believed they were in charge of Guernsey. So we have been greatly influenced by both the French and the English. Later, of course, the Bailiwick of Guernsey – the correct name for the islands including Alderney, Herm and Sark and many other smaller islands and islets – was occupied by German troops in the Second World War. In the First World War, more than 3,000 Guernsey men fought for the British forces, many in the Royal Guernsey Light Infantry.

A lot of the old fortifications from 1940–45 remain around the island as does the famous old Hauteville House, now a museum run by the city of Paris in St Peter Port and where the great French writer Victor Hugo lived after being banished from France. It was there that he wrote *Les Miserables*, one of his greatest works.

Like Hugo I draw inspiration from Guernsey and believe it is an important part of what makes me tick. On a Saturday night on the island, there is a local meat draw when fishermen and local folk come in to buy and sell their fish. It has its own, absolutely wonderful atmosphere. You are there with the guys who are growing vegetables and flowers and with people who go out fishing and work physically every day of their lives.

One of my favourite places to visit is our local pub, The Imperial. We call it 'The Imp' and the nickname suits the place – laid-back, natural and genuine Guernsey. I like it there. Very few people talk to me about motor racing and they just let me enjoy a beer. And I have to say that is a real luxury for me! One particular story perfectly illustrates the warmth of the place. In 1999, fellow racing driver and close friend Darren Manning flew over from Las Vegas to visit. And I took him down to The Imp. He had not been in the pub for long before he exclaimed: 'Wow, this is just fantastic … this tops Vegas!'

The pace of life is also idyllic. Guernsey is not a crowded island so if I have to wait for more than five minutes in traffic it would upset me – never mind the long, slow delays many people live with in London or other big cities. My family loves the place, too. We all have a very natural way of life there. My kids play football outside all day long and we will then have a barbecue. The weather is pleasant and that helps us all lead an active, outdoors lifestyle. My family means more to me than anything else. I am lucky because I usually cannot wait to go to a race or a test, but as soon as it is over I can't wait to get home. It's like having a perpetual enthusiasm for life and I do appreciate it.

I would hate to have got to the top of the mountain and have to live there on my own, unable to share it with anybody. That is why Jo is so important to me, as are the kids, Seb and Dannii, who have given me my values and goals. Sometimes, I might get a phone call from Seb when I am away racing on the other side of the world. He will say: 'Daddy, you are the best – we love you.' To get in my racing car, with that message in my head and the feelings it gives me, is so special. It really helps me find something from within.

And I can feel the Guernsey people behind me when I am racing. I get lovely inspirational emails and letters from them and that gives me confidence, energy and inspiration. You might say I have my own source of people power!

I once used a great technique to draw out some of that Guernsey magic. It was just before I flew to Macau in 2006 to defend my World Touring Car Championship crown from the previous season. And I used it again for my third world title showdown in 2007. It was a very simple thing but a hugely important part of my mental preparation for events that, at the time, were massively demanding challenges.

While still at home in Guernsey I went to the beach with a cup of tea. It was low tide so I could walk on the sand if I wanted. Wanted? I needed to! I took off my shoes, stared at the sea and gave over all my worries to the earth. I just imagined them coming out of my body. Then, I absorbed all the beauty and the strength of the place and felt a real buzz.

I took that with me to Macau. Anytime I felt challenged, I closed my eyes and felt the Guernsey earth and the sand between my toes, the smell of the sea – and that feeling. It really gave me inspiration. Just to swim in the sea, or to go out there on your own in a kayak, and to feel the salt water on your face … That burning feeling when you have just been outdoors in the sun and when you have truly experienced the elements … I just love it.

People have sometimes asked me why I returned after Silverstone and, when I began to earn some decent money, why I did not emulate many racing drivers by moving to Monte Carlo. Well, the answer has always been easy: I knew that Guernsey was right for me, full stop.

Monaco is not my kind of place. It is great for tax reasons, but I also know you would have to live in a little apartment, maybe with a sea view out of only one window

– at least that is what I would end up with! Most people who live there are stinking rich and, as far as I can tell, not like the kind of natural people we have in Guernsey. By saying that I do not mean they are not nice – they probably are, but their attitude to life seems so different.

All the racing drivers I know who live in Monte Carlo spend time there, of course, because they have to for tax purposes, but not all their time. In fact, I am not sure whether they feel as if it is home for them. Monaco can be a great place to visit and it is very glamorous in its own way, but that kind of glamour has never really appealed to me. I guess I have different priorities in my life.

There are other sources of inspiration, too. Being an islander I am a big fan of the sea and to get the most out of it there is nothing better than a boat. It offers pure escapism. The name of my boat is *Flamingo* – apparently it's bad luck to change the name and that is the name I inherited. The boat is nothing special, just a little motor cruiser, and I like to think of it as my floating garden shed! Sometimes, when I need to get away from things, I will just go down to the port and polish it. Most of all, I love taking my family out and seeing them swim off the back of the boat.

I also enjoy the navigational 'challenge' offered by the seas around Guernsey and the Channel Islands. And when I say challenge I mean it. If you can navigate there with all the different currents and tidal streams you can navigate anywhere in the world. The rise and fall of the tide is more than nine metres sometimes – it is definitely a place you have to respect, very much like you have to respect a racing car.

In terms of inspiration I have been enthused by a lot of people in motor racing but struck by only a few. The most inspiring of all has to have been Formula One legend Ayrton Senna. Lots of drivers quote him as their inspiration and role model for not only was he a fantastic driver but a great human being.

I remember the weekend when he was killed in the San Marino Grand Prix at Imola in 1994 so clearly it seems like yesterday. It was a strange situation because I was racing with a guy called Mark Colton that year. We were competing in the Prescott hillclimb, and after Mark had won he made a speech in which he said how sad he was to hear about Senna. We all were, of course. Everyone was simply shocked and stunned. It was one of those moments when your heart beats harder and your whole being is affected.

Anyway, the following year, Mark was killed in a racing accident, too. It was shocking and spooky because Mark was someone who looked very much like Ayrton. That was a time when there were several racing deaths and, after going a long period without any, the sport seemed dangerous again.

I was living at the time in Les Landes, in the Forest, a district of Guernsey in the south part of the island. One day I stopped and looked out to sea, and was thinking about Ayrton and Mark. It was in the run-up to an important race of mine and I had an inspirational moment. It is difficult to explain but I felt the universe in a special way and felt something come into my body. All my hair stood on end and I said to myself: 'Yeah, I am going to go out and do this. I am going to really make this happen.' And I did. I have learned since that if you can draw on times like that, keep the experience and the feeling, then you can get through all the hard times.

I have also been inspired by other drivers, particularly Nigel Mansell who had to work for everything he achieved. He had a very strong supporter, too, in his wife, Rosanne. They worked together as a team, a bit like me and Jo. I remember vividly the epic 1987 British Grand Prix at Silverstone when Mansell raced Nelson Piquet wheel-to-wheel and won. He was such a racer! But it was Mansell's guts, the determination and the commitment I was most impressed by – he worked so hard, just like me. The legendary Stirling Moss was another inspiration – he was pure class in a racing car.

As a racing driver I am often asked about my thoughts on mortality – what I think about life and death, or the risks I am take every time I climb into my car at a race track. Senna was arguably the greatest driver of all time yet people say that if he can be killed it can happen to anybody, and that is so true.

But I am like a lot of people with a dangerous job. I know tragedy can happen, but I do not allow myself to think about it. We all have fear and many times I've worried that I might get killed in a race. But I dismiss it. I call that 'my monkey mind'.

Fear is something you have to live with but something you learn to ignore. I tell myself that f-e-a-r stands for 'false evidence appearing real'. I have learned to overcome these obstacles in my mind by doing all I can to banish them, and working instead to concentrate on positive goals, and things that I can influence and want to achieve.

I believe life should be lived to the maximum. And I cannot see any point in thinking any other way. I want to win, so I think about victory. I want to weep tears of joy and feel utterly happy, so I think of that joy and that happiness. Negatives from my monkey mind are banished. That said, I do not know how I would deal with the situation if Seb or Dannii told me they wanted to go racing. I would prefer it if Seb in particular wanted to be a footballer – it is less dangerous and much cheaper for the parents!

It costs millions to have a motor racing career. And it is very risky. I read about the top-paid footballers and think:

'Yes, Seb, go for it, son!' Seriously, who said that Jo and I do not care about money? After all, we know the value of a good life.

5 SURVIVAL OF THE FITTEST

'I took up karate and started watching karate films. I was trying to learn how to fend for myself.'

I WAS BULLIED AT SCHOOL. Not right at the beginning but when I was a teenager. It was hard. I suffered from mental, verbal and physical abuse on a regular basis and it hurt. But I learned how to rise above it and prove myself. I did not tell anyone at the time and while I would never wish it on anyone else it did teach me a few things and I learned how to tough it out. Maybe that is where my real grit came from.

Physically I was quite small compared to a lot of the boys at school and I lacked some confidence because of that. But I was pretty tough, fit and active, and I was not scared. I think a lot of the attributes I picked up as a kid by tearing around on anything that moved and playing a lot of sport served me well later on. I can certainly see that now even if it did give my mother, Judy, cause for worry in those days.

I do not think I suffered any serious trouble when I went to St Martin's Primary School, aged just four, in 1977. I was just an ordinary kid who was into skateboarding and had a lot of enthusiasm for motorised vehicles of any sort. By the age of five I was riding a 50cc Italjet motorbike. Soon after that I was into karts, then bikes, motorbikes, indeed anything quick and dangerous.

I was crazy about them. Forget school or library books, I read only magazines about speed, racing or bikes. By the time I was ten I was also a keen mechanic. I used to wear a pair of red racing overalls to help my dad, Graham, with his race preparations. He was a racing ace, just like my granddad, Skip, who used to race his home-prepared six-cylinder yellow Chrysler on Vazon sands in the 1940s. Racing was in the blood. And, in a way, that was part of the cause of my problems at school.

I failed my 11-plus, but managed to pass the entrance exam to gain a place at Elizabeth College for Boys in St Peter Port in 1984. It should have been the making of me but I just was not made for classrooms and books. I was born to be outdoors, to work on cars or bikes and to play sport. Having said that, the first two or three years at the college were great and, so far as it is possible at school, I think I enjoyed myself.

Then a close friend of mine had a really nasty accident riding my motorbike, a 100cc Yamaha RXS, and badly hurt himself. It appeared to other people that my motorbike was the cause of the accident, although that was not true. He just could not handle the bike.

I had the motorbike when I was fourteen, a young age for Guernsey, and I was one of the few kids who owned one. I was racing motocross at the time so felt confident on a bike.

My friend asked me if he could ride my bike. He was in my year and, although older than me, was a much less experienced rider. His mum did not know anything about it.

He had a licence so I expected him to have some understanding of what to do. But instead of just having a nice slow ride and feeling his way, he went absolutely mad. He went off very fast and ended up slamming flat-out into a hedge. He was seriously injured.

Obviously I felt awful about it. I do not know if he blamed me but his family tried to and it was all very difficult. They tried to accuse us of negligence which was unfair. They said the brakes were not right, and this and that were wrong and so on, even though the bike was fine. Our family has always taken great care of our bikes, cars, karts and everything else. My dad has always been a stickler for that kind of thing – after all it was his business to run cars. And I am the same: I like things looked after properly.

Anyway, the whole affair ended up in court and, of course, it became a bit ugly. In the end, I was acquitted of all blame for the accident. It had not been my fault and there had been no mechanical failure. It was just a rider error.

However, there was a lot of bad feeling afterwards. I think it was partly because I had a motorbike at that age while some of the others did not – and I think some parents resented that, perhaps out of jealousy. My friend, who recovered thankfully, appeared as if he wanted to turn everybody against me. For at least a year it was an awful time at school.

First of all, the other kids started to take the mickey out of my family, particularly my dad. When you are a young lad at the impressionable age of fourteen, all that stuff is very hurtful. My dad was a well-known figure because of his business and lifestyle, and it was unfair that they should pick on me for that. Yet it developed further from there.

It ended up with me being pushed around quite a bit. I soon realised I would have to stand up for myself. I needed to toughen up fast. Things got so bad that I was going into school not knowing if I would come out with a black eye or whether I would get through the day okay.

On one particular evening the bullies sent a whole load of Chinese and Indian takeaway food to our family's house. But I did not make a fuss and tell my parents anything. Another time, I was in the school tuck shop and got hit by some guy and pushed into a fridge. It was an awful time and left me feeling very isolated, which was the worst part, and it took me quite a while to recover.

By making me withdraw it led me into a lifestyle choice that, on reflection, was an important reason for my going into motor racing. I had started making friends outside of school through racing motorbikes and those guys were really great.

I took up karate and started watching karate films. I was trying to learn how to fend for myself. I did that for about two years until I left school and I became pretty good. As a result, I have decided I want my own son, Seb, to try karate at an early age – he might need self-defence skills one day. More than that, it breeds confidence and inner-strength, and that is important.

When I look back now, I see that unhappy school time as a real positive because if you can come through that situation and still be determined, well, then you can handle anything. I never let it stop me believing in what I wanted to do. I do not actually think the bullying was my own fault, although maybe at that time I was a cocky little schoolboy who did get up a few noses! But I definitely learnt from that experience – not to be arrogant, egotistical or stand out too much. Better to stay in the crowd and look after yourself.

Those experiences, and the mental scarring they left, also influenced me quite a bit at the beginning of my racing career because I felt I did not want to 'puff myself up' too much. On the other hand, it made me knuckle down and try even harder with my driving when things got tough.

My early life in Guernsey was not all bad though, save for those couple of years. I had a great childhood with a real sense of freedom and lots of love. I adored going outdoors and tearing around. We lived in a very modest house in a cul-de-sac in St Martin's where I could enjoy myself doing anything I wanted and I loved all sport and adventure.

I always craved excitement and enjoyed taking risks. My mum remembered one story about a magician who visited Guernsey. Apparently, he saw me doing my thing and told her that he thought I'd got 'something special'.

Dad remembered it too. So, for the sake of accuracy and to prove how diligent I have been in researching this book, I asked both him and my mum about it. 'His name was John Calbert,' Dad recalled. 'He was a professional magician and showman, one of those guys who go floating round the world. He would ask you the time and, as quick as that, your watch was gone!

'He was amazing like that. He once drove up Val des Terres – a famous Guernsey hillclimb – blindfolded! Anyway, he came to see us at the garage once and said to Judy, "This young boy is going to be special and something special is going to happen to him in the future …"' I was just three years old at the time!

It is probably a good thing I never knew anything about that when I was younger. I was a bad enough tear-about as it was. If I believed I had more supernatural powers than I had already invented for myself, who knows what would have happened. As it was, I was always having scrapes, small accidents and frightening the life out of my mum.

There was one particular occasion when I fell out of the tree in the St Martin's School playground – my friends have always reminded me of this – and I crashed to the ground. I got up and ran around shouting, 'I'm paralysed! I'm paralysed!' I was about five or six at the time. It is a big family joke now, of course, but I suppose it must have been a funny incident at the time. It is fair to say that I always have been a little bit sensitive about my health.

My sister Fiona certainly recalls that story and quite a few others about our childhood. We are, and always have been, pretty close and remain good friends. It is great to have that kind of support. We are now both married with our own families but share fond memories of our child-hoods.

Mine began when I was born on 8 August 1973 at the Princess Elizabeth Hospital in Guernsey. My mum, whose maiden name was Short, was one of four girls and my dad one of four, too, although not all boys. Everyone always said that Fi (Fiona) and me were like twins born with a three-year age gap. We laugh at the same things and finish each other's sentences. That kind of thing sticks forever so we must have grown up close.

When we were very young we lived in Beau-Rivage in Torteval where, according to Fi, I went to a toddlers group. She told me the group was held in the same parish as our house but I always cried and never wanted to leave my mum to go there. It seems as if I always preferred a life outside the classroom. Then, from the age of four until about ten, I attended St Martin's. I liked it there, but again, thanks to Fi, I am told I was always very anxious about being picked up on time at the end of the day. Apparently, it was always: 'Oh, where's mum? Has she had a crash? Is she coming to get me?'

At home I was more interested in motorbikes than anything else. I had a little 50cc Italjet motorbike with a two-stroke engine. It was an automatic and I grew up on the thing. I have clear memories of looking through motor-

Aged 5 and on my first motorbike, an Italjet 50cc, in the road outside the family home.

I took over my Dad's garage from an early age with my kart. The rear wheel of his Tiga Sports race car can be seen in the background.

Below Seb and Dannii, our little miracles.

Above Like father like son. Seb at my best mate's wedding.

Above The boys at the motocross club, with me always Number 80.

Left Great fun and lots of mud at a motocross event.

My granddad Skip's 'flying banana' on the sand at Vazon in Guernsey.

My first race car, the legendary Mallock U2.

Above My Dad paid a piper at Doune to celebrate my win in the 1995 British Hillclimb Championship.

Left The happiest day of my life. A winter Christmas wedding was the only time Jo and I could squeeze it in!

My 'prize' drive – Formula 1 at last!

Me and Chris Cramer: 100% commitment, 100% restraint.

A very tiny Seb.

Below The generation gap: my granny Blanche and Seb at his christening.

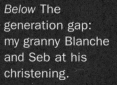

Above My home, my office, my life – all in one little caravan.

I think my name on the intake meant
the most to me; thanks Mario, Frank
and the team.

Andy Priaulx
(GBR)
BMW Team UK
BMW 320si

1

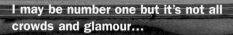

I may be number one but it's not all crowds and glamour...

Left Me and my twin (not quite) sister Fi. I love you, Fufty!

Mum and Dad, my longest suffering supporters.

Left Jo and I celebrating my WTCC title, 007 style.

Below The only time you might get a word in; this story got me more national press than winning the World title.

At home on the water. Scb, Dannii and their cousin Jake on a rare day off for me.

Right The flying
Mygale, Formula
Renault, Thruxton,
1996.

Below I love
autographs – and
look at all the
sponsors' badges
on my overalls!

Silverstone 1998
and my first
Spider drive.

bike books and rummaging around tools, and trying to work out how I could build one. I have always loved motor-bikes and remember thinking: 'How can I carve a motor-bike out of wood?' I was always thinking about things like that – even at just four years old. I used to jump my little motorbike off the pavements and make ramps or go flat out tearing up and down the cul-de-sac – I do not know how the neighbours coped. But it does help to explain how I developed my early love of speed, my balance and strength, and a bit of the courage you need to go racing.

I did not need a lot of teaching either. My dad said I learned my skills by hanging on to a basket on a bike for ten or fifteen minutes and then he'd let me go. To me, it was all so easy and natural.

Although I was not a big boy, I was naturally athletic and dubbed 'Pigeon Chest' – because I did not have much of one on me! I rode motocross even though I could hardly touch the pedals. But I won races, just by hanging off the back of this bike with the throttle wide open.

There were accidents, of course. Fi remembers them better than I do. And she should because – and I'm sure she won't mind my saying – she was always a bit of a tomboy. I used to persuade her to do jumps on her motocross bike with me. One day she jumped and crashed just under a trailer. It was a bit of a heart-stopping moment, especially as Fi was not wearing a helmet. She recalled that mum and dad were very upset, particularly as they did not know what we were doing.

She also reminded me of another incident when I was six and scraped my fingernails rather badly on Christmas Eve. We were supposed to be getting ready to go into St Peter Port to see Father Christmas. We were looking forward to it but we ended up going to the hospital with me as the patient after I'd had the accident. I was on my motocross bike, racing round our field close to home, and I sailed much too close to a wall, scraping my fingernails and causing quite a lot of damage. Suffice to say I was none too popular.

My mum remembered the incident well: 'It was horrendous. And he didn't have any gloves on. He just went too close up against a brick wall that was horribly rough and awful. He had a few near misses with his bike. And Fiona was nearly as bad ...'

Interestingly, my mum reckoned I was 'a nervous child really, scared of blood and that sort of thing' and has told people she 'cannot understand why he's doing this motor racing – it's obviously a balancing act, as if he's not actually worried about himself getting hurt.' I have thought about that and still do not know. Maybe she knows more about me than I know myself.

At that tender age, my mum had to buy me motorbike magazines because I would not read anything else. Oh, and I went to bed with my skateboard. Our little cul-de-sac was perfect for skateboarding and brilliant, too, for that little Italjet bike. I also learned a few tricks, the way boys do when they are growing up like that.

I used to wear my roller-skates as I rode the Italjet flat out up and down the road with the front wheel in the air. It was wonderful! I was into all kinds of things as a toddler: Meccano, Action Man, cars, BMX bikes, Evel Knievel and so on. I also vividly remember my first go-kart which I took to immediately.

One of the great things about Guernsey is the many hills and fun places to go. I used to take my little wooden kart down to this fantastic hill, called Le Val, in the local area. And I remember how the other kids could hardly believe it when I went right to the top and all the way down. I came out of a left-hander with complete opposite lock, drifting the kart down the hill on my first go. I can see the wheel now and the ropes I was pulling ...

One time, a family friend came over from the UK and ended up in hospital because he had tried to copy all the things I was doing. I have been lucky to have a natural sense of balance allied to very little fear. Indeed, not long ago, when I was on a skiing trip, our instructor told me: 'You ski better than Michael Schumacher!' And she meant it.

My dad and granddad were the same. My dad told me we all had the same kind of 'good eye' for judgement. He can remember, he said, seeing his father unbelievably riding a pushbike backwards while sitting on the handle-bars ...

This kind of thing may seem strange but it helped me understand my own fascination with all kinds of vehicles. I have a good friend, or rather *we* have a good family friend, called Darren Manning with whom I learned to ride a unicycle while at Speedsport in my early Formula Three days. That is not a normal activity really, is it? So I guess it adds to the belief that I was one of those people blessed with an unusual sense of balance and a taste for risk. Anyway, I remember all the crashing into bins and other objects as we learned to handle it. When you think back to my granddad's penchant for sliding cars around on the beach, it is easy to see where all this came from.

I grew up hearing all the stories about my family's racing exploits in sand racing – not, as my dad corrected me, beach racing. Sand racing is a real Guernsey activity. The racers would wait for the tide to go out about half a mile and then lay out a loosely marked track on the wet sands. They would then invite people to come down and enjoy the racing. I loved the stories – and when I was four-teen and old enough I had a go, racing motorbikes on the beaches at Vazon.

My childhood days were full of a wide range of sporting interests as well. I remember, for example, triumphing in a 'slow bicycle race' by a country mile – that's an event in which you just balance on the bike and the last person to cross the finish line wins. It is not as easy as it sounds. You really have to hang on in there. I also recall winning hands down a skipping race at the local school sports day. I just ran flat out and that was it.

One teacher, a Mrs Mahy at St Martin's School, told me I should be in a cage at the back of the class. She must have thought I was a bit of an 'outdoors' nuisance to the rest of the school. I just was not the academic type. I was the boy who sat in the classroom, my chin resting on my hand, while my eyes were focused on the outdoors to see what was going on. I just could not settle down to being an 'indoors' person.

Thankfully, we had another teacher, old Mrs Plant, who did believe I had a brain and some kind of talent. She was the wife of Phil Read, the legendary motorcyclist, known as 'The Prince of Speed' and who twice won the 500cc World Championship, in 1973 and 1974. No wonder I felt more affinity with her – she probably knew a lot about motorbikes and racing. She actually said one day – though I may not have any witnesses to this – that she thought I was *quite* intelligent! Praise indeed for Priaulx.

The trouble was that I just was not interested in most of the schoolwork. I did become interested in note taking, computers and writing because they were the kind of skills that I could see would be useful one day. So they drew my attention.

However, lest I have given completely the wrong impression, there were some things at school that I did well. I did have to work hard at school, certainly at a lot of things, and I was involved in the Combined Cadet Force, which provided good training, and I was also good at gym and sport. I was an army boy and could climb ropes and jump over walls better than anyone else. The school said I was a real 'squaddie' – short, stocky and fast.

I think I was average academically but the college was full of clever people, many high-flyers destined to have professional careers as doctors and lawyers. I was doing a lot of stuff outside school, such as karting and motocross, and I do not think too many others were doing the same kind of thing.

Looking back now, I regret not being serious about my schoolwork. My mother was always encouraging as was my dad although he was also very busy trying to make ends meet with his work and various other projects. Needless to say, Fiona was perfect!

In the end, I somehow survived school. I was not happy at the college when I was a teenager and growing up. I escaped from both that and the bullying into my other world of motorbikes and motocross. I did my five years, but I was certainly not a model student. I can remember when we were preparing to take our GCSE exams and supposed to be on study leave at home; I was actually working at a shop on Market Street called Street Life, selling clothes.

At that time, in my mid-teens, I was living my life in my own way. I used to wear the wrong clothes and even had an earring. I think you get the picture ...

I did take part in the school-release work experience scheme and managed to get myself a job as a technician with a BMW dealer. It was ideal and I loved it. I negotiated to turn it into a holiday job – so hopefully when I came to leave school I would have a job lined up. I left the college in July 1989 aged 16 and started work on a five-year apprenticeship at Jacksons, the BMW dealer based in Forest.

I think my mother was concerned for me, however. Of course, she always wanted the best for me. When I asked her what she remembered of my schooldays, she told me: 'You didn't like school really, you didn't concentrate on your homework or anything like that. You were only interested in the sporty side and musically you played the clarinet. You had a good singing voice, good enough to be in the choir. As I played the piano, we tried to get you to learn as well but that was too slow. You always wanted to do things so quickly that you never gave yourself time.

'And you hardly did any reading at all. I'd stand over you, otherwise I do not think you would have read anything at all. The teachers just told me: "Get him to read anything" so we would buy magazines on motorbikes and cars, and just let you read those. That's about the only thing that held your interest and concentration. I wasn't really aware that you weren't particularly happy at the time – it certainly didn't show. I thought you had a lot of friends. You seemed to be very popular ...'

She did not know about the bullying which was probably just as well. I am determined to ensure my children do not suffer like that. I also hope that, in some way, my example can teach people there is a way that each of us can achieve things in life. It takes hard work, grit and some courage, yes, but it can be done. Those bullies were never going to stop me.

6 FAMILY MATTERS

'My dad put all his money into me … But I am sure my career has made him stop and think about his own missed opportunities and that, for a while, was something that stood between us.'

WE ARE A CLOSE-KNIT LOT. And, like most families in Guernsey, we are hard working and down-to-earth. I would never say we are anything special. I like to keep myself on a level with everyone around me and that ethos derives from my family background. My granddad, Skip, was a real grafter who took a chance after the Second World War and started selling cars in Guernsey. My dad followed him into the business and I would have done the same had I not been tempted away by motor racing – which just happened to be both my grandfather and my father's favourite activity away from work. They loved the sand racing and the hillclimbs and, as you would expect in a place like Guernsey, they grew up loving the sea and boats as well.

The Priaulx surname is one of the oldest in Guernsey, but we are not a posh family, just a well-established clan –

indeed our name can be traced as far back as William the Conqueror from the eleventh century, so that is a long time! My paternal granddad was actually named Ernold and he and my grandmother, Blanche, had four children. My dad, Graham, was the oldest son and married my mum, Judy Short, whose father was a master butcher. My maternal grandmother also ran the local post office, so there were a lot of enterprising people around me as I grew up.

Not only is my mum's side of the family musical but they also live a long time. It is no exaggeration to say they often live well into their nineties and sometimes even longer. So I'll be around a while yet, if I am lucky. We are all, of course, Guernsey people, and the island way of life and old traditions have helped ensure we look after one another and are careful about how we live. We take risks, just like anyone else does, but maybe calculate things a bit more carefully.

My sister, Fiona, is my 'twin', although she's three years younger than me. She knows how I tick because, when we were younger, she was often outside with me doing the same crazy things as me on bikes and karts. We were close as kids and have remained in regular touch even though we are now both married with families. I am lucky in that we all live within easy reach of each other on the island so it is quite normal for us to share meals together. It is one of my best reasons for my living back in Guernsey even though it does mean a lot of travel when I have to attend sponsors' functions, testing or race meetings all over the world.

I grew up to understand the value of hard work and how important it was to look after things properly. Cars, obviously, but also tools and other bits of equipment were always highly valued by my dad. You only have to see the inside of his garage at home to see what I mean. Everything has its place and it's so clean you could eat your dinner off the floor.

Dad did everything for us as we grew up and made sure we never went without anything. He was always very busy, and sometimes a bit of a 'part-timer' with his kids because he was so committed to his business, but my mum made up for any time we missed out on with him. When dad was around, though, he always gave us his full attention. In some ways, I am the same with my family. My work sometimes takes me away for weeks at a time and I rely completely on Jo, my wife, to look after the kids, Seb and Dannii, and keep the home safe and sound. Again, she is fortunate because both our families are just a few minutes' drive away from our home.

I love to ring home and hear all the family voices. It can be quite stressful at times, to travel so much and be away for so long, but my phone calls home, and my closeness to everyone, is a real source of comfort. I believe so much in my family and they are one of my greatest strengths.

My dad, without doubt, is the man most responsible for my successful racing career. I could not have done it without him. Firstly, he brought me up; secondly, he introduced me to the motor trade, and taught me how to sell and do deals; and, thirdly, he supplied the support and, more often than not, the financial backing I needed to keep racing when times were tough.

When I was growing up, dad and me were really great friends, and I had total confidence and belief in him. But as I grew older and went through my own life experiences, I began to see things more in my own way. I remember someone once telling me that when my dad turned 50 he would change and become more difficult. Well, when he reached that milestone he did actually become a little more different and definitely more like hard work. But then, maybe, I was just as bad at the time. We were not so close as I grew older; he had his pressures just as I had mine. I just had to stand back and take stock, and that is partly why I ended up doing my own thing and leaving Guernsey back in 1997.

I also think he was frustrated with me because he saw the talent I had as a racing driver and, as year followed year, he probably realised he was not going to have the resources to keep funding me. I am not being ungrateful, but a car salesman in Guernsey is not going to enjoy the kind of multi-millionaire lifestyle that would enable him to fund his son to do whatever he wants in his career.

In the early days, we were talking £15,000 a year to cover the hillclimbing costs for a whole season. That was difficult enough, but when I was looking to break away into Formula Three the stakes became much higher. Suddenly we had to find fifteen grand for just one test.

There was no doubt in my mind I had the potential and ambition to succeed but it heaped a lot of pressure on my dad. I have to say, in fairness, that he never made it seem like an unrealistic target but, sadly for both of us, he could not really help me any further with funding.

So when I left school, and following my spell with the BMW dealership, I went to work for my dad. It made sense. But there was always tension and, at that time, it was becoming tougher than ever to succeed in the motor trade in Guernsey. That, of course, is one of the negatives of living on an island: you have a ceiling on the size of your local market.

That said, my granddad had been a bit of a pioneer and sold Fiats in Guernsey after the Second World War. Indeed, to even sell Italian cars on the island was an amazing feat. And he worked hard at selling them well.

He would often drive a car to a potential customer's house, end up selling it and then walking home. That, for me, was real determination and shows the kind of grit you need to succeed in your career. He built up his business – Forest Road Garage – by himself and my father later introduced Ferrari and Alfa Romeo to Guernsey. Dad eventually took over from granddad – he acted as managing director of granddad's company before selling it to help fund Skip's retirement and branching out on his own – and was himself successful in the trade having learned a lot from him.

Anyway, by the time we reached the early to mid Nineties, when I was really keen to do more racing, trade-wise things were changing in Guernsey quite a bit. My dad had enjoyed a successful time with his business, Graham Priaulx Car Sales, but as time passed an increasing number of rival garages opened in Guernsey.

This influx of competition made life more difficult for dad. Indeed, a new business was opened directly opposite ours so customers would come to us and then go to that one as well. We were struggling at a time when I really needed things to be going well for my career's sake. Financially, 1995 was a tough year because I was still working as a car salesman while harbouring big ambitions to be a racing driver.

At around this time my granddad became ill and that had a big effect on my outlook on life. He meant a lot to me but when I saw him lying in hospital it made me doubly determined to do something positive with my life.

It was at that time things really came to a head. It was difficult, being away so much racing, to give the business my total commitment – yet I know I should have been around more because trade was not great and we had a crisis on our hands. Dad had given me an opportunity for which I will always be grateful, but it was never going to be my future. And this is where Jo comes in …

Jo and I had become engaged in 1993 and bought our first house that year. I needed her support and we were desperate for some good business ideas. We worked out that the best thing would be to take a plot of land at the garage and sell cars ourselves. My dad had helped us sort out a mortgage for the house. But we had to raise some money ourselves in order to get our own little business venture off the ground.

After all that my dad had done for us already I now found myself leaning on Jo's parents. They gave us £2,000 to buy a car and then sell it on. It was a beautifully minted Peugeot 205 that we later sold. We were on our way. Our turnover grew and we worked hard to make the business a success although it was not that long ago that I was able to pay them back. It costs so much money to go motor racing that every driver accumulates a lot of debts, mainly from borrowings, along the way and you can only settle them when you have found some success.

We sold 11 cars in one month during 1992! That may not sound a lot to someone with a vast dealership or two in England, but for Guernsey that was a good four week's work. It was what we needed. We were borrowing money to go racing and I had to sell a lot of cars each month to settle the repayments. There I was, only around 19 years old, and I was wheeling and dealing to survive. Even now, after winning three world touring car titles, I am the same. No wonder former Formula One driver Derek Warwick, who has been a real mate in support of my career with lots of good advice, once berated me: 'Priaulx, stop being such a wheeler-dealer – you are a world champion!' But I cannot help myself – I am always doing deals. Anyway, I think Derek is the same …

My dad was talking me through deals all the time yet so much conflict existed between us, too. Our relationship has, at times, been a difficult one but there is still a lot of respect and affection there. We support each other and now, as he is growing older, I think he can enjoy, and appreciate, my success. I am glad of that.

Back in the sixties my dad was offered a drive with Mini Cooper but declined in order to work in the family business. Perhaps that has grated with him a little, yet he has lived a lot of his life through me and has enjoyed the travel, some great races and, I'm sure, has taken pride in my championship successes. He is a proud man and has lived a very active life. But I believe he found it difficult to grow older and see me enjoy the limelight he perhaps could have had himself. I am sure he was proud of me, but he may also have felt something for himself.

As people we can be very different, too. For example, my dad's attitude to helping with the housework is to lift up his feet a bit when my mum is going round with a vacuum cleaner. Yet I am much more hands-on with housework and everything when I am at home.

I believe it's a pity that because some people in Guernsey thought we were a wealthy family, a lot of things were misunderstood. I am sure it contributed to the bullying I suffered at school. My dad enjoyed his life and spending his money. He was comfortably well off for a man in Guernsey, but not rich, and neither am I – even though now I am able to say, at last, that I have some money in the bank.

In fact, many people in Guernsey believe all my racing has been paid for by my family when it has not been, and that I am the lucky boy with a silver spoon in my mouth – yet that is just not true.

Right from the start, my family supported me, but we never had the big piles of cash it takes to fund a serious career in motorsport. When I was hillclimbing it really was a family affair with a motorhome and lots of fun. And the family attended most of the races when I was competing in Renault Spiders. Indeed, Jo's family has learned about a whole different life through my racing. My mum enjoyed it, too, although she does not travel so much now. She and her sister, my aunt Sue, share a bookkeeping business and that, together with her music and church interests, keeps her occupied these days.

When I asked my mum about the early days, she smiled and recalled: 'Look at all the fun we had! You can't put a price on the people we have met and the things that we've seen. It's another world really, isn't it? Only I can't comprehend it fully now, when you go away and all the cameras are around you … I think: "Oh, that's my son. It's amazing."'

Although I am very much like my mum in many ways, she knows me well and can say anything to me. And she could always tell if I was trying to bunk off school by claiming I wasn't feeling well or if I was genuinely ill. I was naughty, but nice, and she knew that. As a family, although some of us have drifted apart a little over the years, I feel we are all becoming much closer once more which is great. I am mellowing and, with my kids growing up fast, there is plenty to think about. That is the nature of family life and I would not change my family for the world.

7 STUBBORN AS A MULE

'Anyway, this red car turned up outside my house – and you had yellow trousers on and turquoise shades! I thought: "This guy's not for me. He's a bit way out!"'

BELIEVE ME, I know I am a lucky bloke.

I have had a lot good fortune in many different ways. I was born in a beautiful place with a wonderful family. I have had some tough times, of course, but was able to find a way of surviving them and turning my problems, and my weaknesses, into things that made me stronger. I was blessed with that kind of grit.

I was so determined – often so stubborn – to succeed that I battled my way through and achieved what I wanted: to have a top-level, world-class career in motorsport. To date I have even managed to win three world championships in succession so I know I have been granted my fair share of fortune in having a bit of talent and relentless determination not to mention a magnificent racing team behind me. That said, I have still worked very hard to achieve my goals.

But my greatest good fortune has been to meet and marry my wife, Jo. I can honestly say I would not have achieved all that I have these last few years had it not been for her.

Jo is my rock. She is, like me, from Guernsey and is possessed of the same values. She does not care one jot for the fake images that seem to matter so much to some people – she just wants to do the best she can for all of us and without any pretence at all. And I know I can rely on her completely.

She is such a strong girl and boasts special qualities. She keeps my feet on the ground and has made me believe in myself. We work so well together and our partnership is at the root of my success.

Fortunately, having a motorhome at a race meeting meant that when they were babies, I could have the children, Seb and Dannii, with Jo and I when I was racing. I could pick them up, have a cuddle, give them a kiss and then go back to the team again.

I find it amazing how readily Jo adapted to the racing life. She is well known around the paddock for her very straightforward way of seeing things and behaving. Sometimes however, it has meant she has been caught hollering 'like a fishwife' during races even when I have warned her that the television cameras will hunt her down …

Jo comes from such a lovely family. Before they met me, I do not think any of them, Jo included, had really ventured away from Guernsey much, if at all. I took Jo out of that bubble completely and she rose to the challenge. And that has been wonderful for me because she now knows, from a racing perspective, what makes me tick. She knows what is right for me and what gets the best out of me.

These small things were always so important to me when we had our own motorhome with us at the races. I won my first Formula Three race at Snetterton in 1991 soon after Seb was born and my family has always seemed to bring me the energy to succeed. It was the same with Dannii. When I was racing in that series in 2002, I saw guys in the British Touring Car Championship buy flash cars like a Ferrari after they had signed their first contract. Me? I bought a motorhome so my family could be closer to me at the races.

That was the advantage of being a relatively late starter. I was mature enough to see things in a way I would not have done when I was just 20 or 21. And a lot of that has been down to Jo, because she has a shrewd head on her shoulders and has worked hard to make ends meet. She knows what it is like to struggle and worry about making the mortgage payments. She has been there and done it with me. And right from the start, maybe because she is a little older than me, she has been able to settle me down, and helped me take myself seriously and become a more responsible person.

Indeed, looking back, I am amazed she put up with me at all! But she has told me that she had never met anyone with as much determination as me, with a kind of relent-lessness that does not go away. I have put everything on the line for my career, and so has Jo, and we were at one time early in my career down to virtually nothing. My dad has helped us a lot, too, because he was always great in seeing the positive side.

When I fell in love with Jo I had the same kind of feel-ings as I had for motor racing – a few butterflies in my stomach and so on – but obviously quite different, too. I do not know why or how these things happen, but I believe if you want something badly enough and you believe in it then it will come true. I felt like that about Jo. And she helped change me from being a boy who was still playing with things to a man whose life had a real structure.

She did not take the fun away from me, or out of me, but she gave me responsibility. I am one of those guys who knows what they want and makes sure they are going to get it. And, as far as Jo was concerned, I was prepared to put my whole life into her and her alone.

Once we were together she was as committed to both the relationship and my career as I was. We knew what my goals were and what sacrifices might have to be made and she went with it all the way. Jo was perhaps a bit railroaded when it came to the idea of leaving Guernsey for England, but I think she knew that she would not be able to stop me.

She also knew, however, that I loved her and wanted her to be with me, so it was not a question of her staying in Guernsey while I went off to England. I would never have allowed that to happen. She had to come with me and we had to do it as a team.

Jo has many qualities, and her family background is responsible for much of that. She has always known about hard work. Her dad, Louis LeTocq, was one of eight children who would be out at three or four o'clock in the morning to prepare and box up the tomatoes or freesias. Being a grower is a very 'hands-on' type of work, and tests your strength and durability. You definitely need character to do that well, day in, day out, and in all weathers. And then who did she bring home one day to meet Louis and Lorna, her hard-working parents? Me, a guy who, at that time, was nothing more than a dreamer.

And you can only imagine what they thought later when their beautiful daughter's daydream-believer of a boyfriend began talking about leaving Guernsey and taking her with him. Actually, we were engaged by the time that happened, but that is another story.

I remember being invited round one Sunday for lunch and there was me, Jo, her brother, Steve, and Helen, his wife, Louis and Lorna. We were sitting together eating and talking away, and everything was fine, when Steve said he had an announcement to make. 'We've got some news,' he told us and revealed Helen was pregnant. Of course, we congratulated them.

Unfortunately, Jo was a bit upset. It was a bombshell moment for us. We were struggling along in our own way, with me working at the garage and going racing while Jo worked for Sarnia Estates as a sales negotiator. But I was not really pulling up any trees or making any real money and Jo was three years older than Helen, which brought matters into sharp focus. Anyway, Lorna just turned and looked at me, and said: 'So, Andy, what are you doing with your life?'

I was really sensitive about that because it was tough for me at the time. It was a pretty pointed question, I felt useless and did not know what to say. So, I just got up, slammed my knife and fork down on the table and walked out, jumped in the car and went home.

It is a rare thing for me to lose control, let alone at a moment like that, and especially in front of Jo's family. I think that episode showed just how much pressure I was putting myself under, and how difficult I was finding it to make ends meet and keep my dream alive.

However, Jo's parents are genuine people who have been there for us all the time. Indeed, I never managed to have an argument with Jo on her own because her mum would always be involved, stepping in and calming her down! Looking back now, I realise she questioned me only because she wanted the best for Jo, as she always has done. Yet I saw it only in terms of myself. Still, Lorna and I have always got along very well – even if she does refuse to watch the Rolling Stones with me!

I first clapped eyes on Jo at a disco at the Golden Monkey in St Peter Port in 1991. I was just a few weeks shy of my 19th birthday. I was a bit of a so-and-so in those days and wore a white tracksuit, as Jo has often reminded me. She was amazed at how I looked, she said. But it did the trick. It definitely caught the eye.

She said she always went for younger guys but I think it was me who was in control. We do not always agree about that, but it was not until quite a few months later that I asked her out for the first time.

I had left school in July 1989, aged 15, and started an apprenticeship at Jacksons Garage, a BMW dealership in Forest, where I learned a lot. The following summer, soon after my seventeenth birthday, I passed my driving test first go. That year, 1990, I also won the Guernsey Motocross Championship in the 250cc class.

Those were colourful years for me growing up in Guernsey. A lot was going on in my adolescent life, but the centre of my world was motocross, motorbikes, and anything to do with cars and speed. I was unlucky in one motocross event at Sorrel Point when I was involved in an accident that saw me fall from my bike and suffer a serious knee injury. A whole pack of guys seemed to ride over me and I do not think I could walk properly after that for ages. It was a setback, too, to my working life because I was unable to continue with the apprenticeship at Jacksons. Around the same time I managed to get glandular fever so, after all that, I was lucky when, in 1991, I started working for my dad at his garage.

In July of that year I bought my first racing car, a Mallock Sports Libre. I entered a few local events and, aged 18, won the local Clubmans Sports Racing Car class with two wins. That August I entered my first hillclimb event at the famous Shelsley Walsh course in Worcestershire, reportedly the world's oldest motorsport venue still in active use. I was on my way although, at that time, I did not realise what I was doing or where I was going.

And Jo? Well, after that night at the disco when I first spotted her, I asked her out but she declined and kept me waiting. She knew I was keen but she was not certain about me. But I kept trying. I sent her flowers and little gifts but it was a long process of battering my head against a wall. Not forever, though.

Of those days, Jo told me: 'You asked me out but I wasn't too sure. I was told a few things like "Don't go out with a Priaulx" but I did not know why. I think people thought the Priaulxs were a bit flash because they competed in motorsport and had a garage. I didn't really know much about them.

'I was a country girl from Torteval in the south of the island. We worked in the fields and in the greenhouses. We were a bit suspicious so I didn't go out with you for a little while. My mum said: "Oh, he's too young – you shouldn't go out with him." But one week I saw you with another girl … Well, that was it – I wanted you, and went out with you after that.

'I remember you said to me: "I'll come and pick you up" and you had a Vauxhall Cavalier. You were a bit of a show-off and a lad at that time, and wanted to show the girls a good time. I said to mum: "This guy's picking me up in an open-top car." I was so excited.

'Anyway, this red car turned up outside my house – and you had yellow trousers on and turquoise shades! I thought: "This guy's not for me. He's a bit way out!" But, from then on, we did not spend a day apart from each other.

'I will always remember meeting your mum for the first time. I used to think she must be a proper daredevil, going on powerboats. But when I got to know her I found out she hated boating! And I recalled in the first year we met your dad taking us out in his Sunseeker. I didn't like boats, but had to pretend I did ...'

Jo and I soon became inseparable. I remembered on that boat trip with my dad she was so straight-legged and did not use her legs as suspension at all, so each time we went over a wave and the boat took off she took off with it!

When I was only 19, I was ready to settle down. I know that seems early, but it just felt right. Indeed, considering I was such an immature lad at school, I grew up fast and went out and got a job at 16.

But it was not unusual for Guernsey people to go to work at 15 or 16 in those days. I find that a lot of my friends in England are 15 years behind me in that way. They are 35 years old and not even thinking of kids or marriage. It is so different.

It probably has something to do with the relatively slow pace of life over here. I have always noticed it most after coming home from a trip abroad. Often what you think will be a ten-second conversation will still be going strong five minutes later in Guernsey – people give of their time so freely.

Jo and I were engaged at the Bouley Bay Hillclimb in Jersey in July 1993. I was not even 20. But I wanted to be with Jo and it was typical that we would become engaged at a hillclimb. She always made me go faster.

The previous September, I had won my first major event outright, the Alderney Hillclimb, where I also broke the hill record. I knew then that I could drive really quickly and so it was a weekend to remember in all sorts of ways.

Our engagement was announced a few months after we had bought our first house together. That was in May 1993 in the small parish of Forest in southern Guernsey. We loved it and changed its name from *Hamilton* to *Crazy Days* because our first dance had been to Gerry Rafferty's 'Baker Street'. It had a tin roof – we could not afford a proper one.

The first time I took Jo hillclimbing was to the Alderney Hillclimb. I won it and afterwards fell asleep feeling pretty proud of myself. Jo insisted, and I still do not believe her, that in my sleep that night I shouted out: 'I'm the hotshot!' Well, she could not keep that to herself and shared that story with the whole paddock. Everyone had a good laugh at my expense and I was called 'hotshot' for quite a while after that.

Still on this subject, I am also reminded that once in the middle of the night I changed all the wheels on our bed because I thought it was a racing car! I was so into my racing I kept going over pit stops in my head to work out how I could save time and do this and that even more quickly than usual. If all that wasn't enough, we were spending the night at someone's house one time, and I apparently jumped up and started sleepwalking, jumping around going 'Ooh uh ooh.' Jo said that I thought I was a gorilla.

Anyway, we stayed in a campsite that weekend in Alderney. One evening, while returning from a night out, and with Jo on the back of my motorbike, I decided to show off a bit and practise my motocross skills. I was weaving in and out of the tents when I caught a tent pole with the foot peg of my bike. The tent promptly collapsed flat on the floor and I could just about make out the people inside wriggling around ...

Luckily – and please don't get me wrong because it's such a lovely place – there is only one thing to do in Alderney and that is get drunk. The people in this tent, or the flattened remains of it, appeared so drunk they did not really seem to care at all. Much to my relief, when the innocent inhabitants finally emerged they were laughing like mad. I had just about got away with it.

We went hillclimbing for years together, going away every couple of weeks, and it seemed as if every bit of money we had was spent on flying away. To help pay for my racing, we used to valet cars for my dad, Graham, in the evenings, sometimes until one o'clock in the morning just so that I had enough money. Jo threw herself into it and made it her life. It was a wonderful time.

When we sold *Crazy Days* and moved out of Guernsey in 1997 everything changed. We got into debt. Jo was working at Sarnia Estates with Noel Le Tissier – no relation to Matt, the footballer but my Mum's brother-in-law – and I marketed the property on their books. It sold in about a week for £145,000. Of course, when we moved back to Guernsey a few years later, it was worth £400,000. I could have kicked myself. I wished we could have found some way to keep it, but it was impossible.

When we bought our first house, Jo used the £10,000 she had saved up from when she was very young towards paying the deposit. She had scraped the money together over the years by essentially not going out much at all. And when she did, because she had to drive everywhere, she did not drink. Jo also used to sell what are called 'sleeve' flowers. There were five in a bunch with 60 bunches making up a box. She was paid 40p a box and did this nearly all her life until she had a decent amount of savings. In fact, when she initially met me she thought I was loaded, although when we went out for dinner the first time I was £400 overdrawn at the bank.

Before we met, Jo had never been out of Guernsey much, only to Jersey and France. And her parents had never eaten a Chinese meal before I came along. They were very traditional, country people who tended to live an old-fashioned life, but they soon came along and enjoyed our motor racing trips.

My very first race was at the motocross track at Pleimont in 1980. It was just fun and excitement for me. I can remember going to watch various motorsport events, like hillclimbs and sprints, with my dad. Sometimes my dad was competing and although he retired for a while when I was young he started again later on. I remember going home from these meetings, jumping into my motorbike gear and setting up a little track that I raced around on my pushbike.

So that kind of competition was definitely in the blood from an early age. I just loved racing. I cannot remember particularly how good I was at the very beginning – it never seemed that important to me, only that it was fun.

There were some scary moments, of course, because all motor racing is dangerous. I remember once in a kart race at Les Val des Terres I got squeezed out at one corner and, with my mum watching, speared off up towards a tree. It was a heart-in-the-mouth moment, but I managed to come away unscathed.

One guy I remember racing against in karts in those early days was Paul Ozanne who was very quick. His dad had been a very good driver in Guernsey before racing in

Formula Renault in England. He did very well but, as is often the case, ran out of money. That has happened to a lot of talented Guernsey people – they simply do not have the required funds to finance a racing career in England.

I am very proud that I sacrificed everything to follow my dream. This is not meant as an implied criticism of anyone else, but I'm sure a lot of people would not have done so.

I owned a share in the car I raced, a Mallock U2 1700cc, but mostly my father paid for the hillclimbing. That was at a time when I was working at dad's garage and would prepare the car before racing it myself. It was a family effort and I learned a lot from those times. I was selling cars and every now and again I would have a little tinker with the racecar. It was interesting to learn all about how it was bolted together and how to set it up for racing. I think that helped me a lot in future years. I understood how brakes worked, how the suspension fitted together and what would happen if you hit a kerb too hard. That has always meant I try not to be too hard on the equipment.

In one of my first Formula Renault tests, for Martello Racing in 1996, I fired the car off into the gravel at Silverstone. Most young drivers would have thrown the steering wheel into the cockpit and headed off towards the garage, but I started to shovel the gravel out of the sidepods and apologised to the guys who collected the car. I felt really guilty about halting the test, partly because I had been used to looking after my own cars and felt some empathy with the team.

Now, as a seasoned racer, that is not a particularly good way to think in motor racing and I am not like that anymore. Sometimes you have to aggressively launch the car over a kerb and not care too much if it breaks because it will most probably be the quickest line through a corner.

I have read that Michael Schumacher had similar early engineering experiences to mine while Damon Hill is another guy who worked his way up from the bottom. That is probably why we connect well. We are not close friends, but always have a good laugh together. It is a strange thing but all my really close friends are engineers and mechanics – just normal guys.

Now, looking at Seb, my little boy, I believe that if he wants to become a professional driver he will have to start down with karting ... and then there's the rest of it. It is mind-blowing. If Seb does go down the conventional route I reckon he would need about £6 million or £7 million worth of funding behind him to get all the way to Formula One. So I think I'll tell him: 'Be a footballer!' After all, you only need a pair of boots ...

8 I AM A RACING DRIVER

'It had been a long struggle and, at times, a miserable one … but now, with a good drive lined up, I was doubly determined to succeed.'

AFTER JO AND I WERE MARRIED in December 1997, we were blissfully happy – and horrendously hard up. Back in Guernsey we had a great time celebrating during the holiday period after the wedding and welcomed in 1998 with a huge sense of optimism. Nothing could beat us or get us down. Things were changing, we were convinced, for the better. Little did I know then that I would be struggling along on £20 a week – and would be giving up my lunch hours to continue the seemingly endless search for sponsors to back me as a racing driver.

I knew it would be tough and I was ready for that. Apart from my good experience gained from my various successes in the British Hillclimb Championship, I had also been to the Winfield Racing School at Magny-Cours, France, in March 1994. That was thanks to my mum paying for the course with a £750 bonus she had received from work. Thanks, mum! The Winfield School had boasted some very famous graduates including four-time World Champion Alain Prost, 1996 World Champion Damon Hill and former Formula One driver Olivier Panis who had all been under the expert tutelage of Mike Knight.

That visit to France had taught me a few valuable lessons and sharpened me up. I won two of that year's national hill-climb events outright and the following year, 1995, I took ten wins and broke eight records as I achieved a maximum points score in the British series. I was driving the same Pilbeam MP54 and it was a lot more than fun – I was fast and consistent, and enjoyed some great results. That year, I was shortlisted for the Autosport/McLaren Driver of the Year Award and offered a drive in Vauxhall Lotus by Paul Stewart Racing. I was only 22 and, knowing I could not raise the necessary cash to take the seat, I turned it down. I wonder how my career would have turned out had I said yes and then worked as hard as possible to find the funds …

Instead, I stayed in Guernsey but the following April my granddad, Skip, fell seriously ill. That year, 1996, and the next were both tough. I ran out of money but at least I had made the right decision to move to England, and the year ended on a high when Jo and I got married.

Unfortunately I could not start the 1998 season because I did not have sufficient money for the Renault

Spider series. Instead, I was working as an instructor at Silverstone while focusing on my race driving. To be honest, I was using my Silverstone job mainly as an opportunity to meet people, such as potential sponsors. Between sessions – and I would be doing around seven a day – I was in my Ford Escort diesel, on the laptop and phoning people in an effort to drum up the necessary cash for racing. I never took lunch.

By now we had by now paid off all my motor racing debts, and with Jo working in the ticket office at Silverstone we decided to stay in the UK and not return home with our tails between our legs. With a small deposit left over for a house, we invested in a little terraced property in nearby Towcester. However, it left me with £20 a week to live on ...

I never thought I lacked the ability to make it as a top-class racing driver so figured that there must be some sort of foolproof method – something everyone else knew of which I was unaware – that was letting me down. So in 1997 and 1998, while working at Silverstone, I made a point of talking to the other instructors.

Several had enjoyed pretty good racing careers. One, John Pratt, had created a bit of a legendary reputation for himself in Formula Ford as a skilful and determined racer. I recall chatting to him about left-foot braking and he had noted I was all over the place. 'Andy, you really need to

concentrate on yourself, your driving, your working methods ...' John told me. He went on for quite a while about
technique, how to race and so on. I admitted to him that I
did not know anything about all that. I just drove the car
as fast as it would go.

So there I had it. The missing ingredient was the right
technique. So John and me did a deal. I paid him out of my
instructor's income to come racing with me as my own
private coach. He watched for two Formula Three races
and provided some valuable advice. It mainly revolved
around simple things like where I was looking when
approaching corners. For instance, I would be looking
directly at the braking point whereas John told me to look
further ahead at the exit because that was where I was
heading. With hillclimbing all my technique had been
geared towards short tracks and tight turns with everything happening right in front of you. To be a success on
circuits, however, I had to extend my line of vision. So I did
– and all of a sudden my lap times came down.

Unfortunately, the two Formula Three races I managed
to find the funds for in 1997 had been and gone before I
linked up with John. So, I was again scratching around for
drives. I had to rely on the sympathy of people like Nick
Jordan and Bob Dance at TOMS for a chance. Bob was my
mechanic – I gave him a pound coin to enlist him. Ah, the
glamour of motorsport! I think Nick and Bob liked the way

I worked and the fact I had come from grassroots motor-sport. They were honest and told me: 'Andy, you'll have a tough time.' I did not have enough money but they gave me the end-of-season test anyway. I guess they felt a bit sorry for me. John Pratt and me worked really hard for this test. We did a bit of karting and had some private tuition at Silverstone. And it worked. When the test at Croft took place I was actually on the pace.

I was up there with Jonny Kane, the 1997 British Formula Three Champion. Everyone else was testing for the prestigious season-ending race at Macau so these were the best guys around and I was up there with them. I drove faster and faster throughout the session and at the end of the test John said: 'Well, there's Jonny Kane's (best) lap time and there's yours.' And they were pretty close! I thought that was amazing.

I think John wanted me to start again from scratch in my career. He said: 'We need to forget about Formula Three. You have to step back into the lower formulae and I need to work with you again.' I can see now how that would have been the best thing for me. Indeed, if I had done what John suggested maybe three years earlier Formula One would have been much more of a realistic aim, but I tried to fly too high too soon.

I received one opportunity to drive for the Renault Spider Jamie Hunter Racing Team at Silverstone and did really well. I was on the pace and, as luck would have it, a guy called Tim Thomson came along to watch. He could see I was not going anywhere yet was still determined to race. After that race, Tim wrote to me and said: 'Andy, I feel really sorry for you. You did well at Silverstone, but things are not happening for you. I would like to offer you an opportunity. I would like to buy you a race car ...'

That was a Renault Spider and it was great to have but I still had to run the car by myself so I went to see the Alan Docking Formula Three team, based at Silverstone. Alan gave me a corner of his workshop where I prepared the car myself. I remembered writing a checklist of all the things I needed: WD40, washers, engine and gearbox oil, everything. By mid-season we were ready to race in the British Renault Spider series. I was always racing in the top half a dozen, but I was driving a car that was not really on the pace. I was building and preparing the thing myself in the evenings after instructing. I was a really just an amateur club driver and hated it, yet it was the only way I could go racing.

I had wanted to be the ultimate professional, so I prepared the car like it was a Formula One machine. I polished it and looked after it, put everything I had into making it as good as possible. But that only made it harder to take when I did a few races and it still was not working. Things were falling off the car and it was tough to accept.

However, I did score some success in the second half of the 1998 season, bagging my first podium finish at Snetterton and rounding off the campaign with a second place finish at Silverstone.

Incidentally, when my granddad, Skip, died in July 1998 I put my race cap and garland from Snetterton into his grave. He had been such an important part of my life.

That end-of-season success had given me the taste for more of the same. So I kept on chasing up any leads I had and eventually I met a guy, David Hughes, at Silverstone who said: 'Hey, you had a really good end to the season, didn't you?' I thanked him and explained it had been really tough and, although we had done well, I did not have lot of money. He told me he worked for a computer company called Psion and offered to ask them for some sponsorship money. We became friends and we managed to negotiate a deal to race another season in Renault Spiders.

Towards the end of the 1998 season, Tim Thomson had said: 'Look, Andy, I'll find a bit more money and put you in the Mardi Gras Renault Spider team. They'll engineer the car. It's a proper race team. You'll just have to get in and drive the thing fast.' Tim has been, alongside Jo, one of the great supporters and architects of my racing career. So, I joined Mardi Gras for the 1999 season and, for the first time, had a proper racing team running me.

While Psion's backing was appreciated, it was not quite enough money, so Tim said: 'I'll give the (1998) car to you – you don't even have to give it back.' So I sold it to Mardi Gras, the cash raised going towards the running costs for 1999, and agreed that all the prize money would go to the Silverstone-based team. I managed to pull in a load of sponsors, too, one being SG Hambros, the private bank, from Guernsey.

To digress slightly, 1998 was the year I started meditating. I had met up with John Pratt again and, over the winter, he told me how meditation really helped him with his racing. I was not in a position to turn my nose up at anything and was prepared to try whatever it took to be a success. I felt down and out, and if meditation could help me I would be right up for it.

So John and I drove north to attend a meditation course. We met up with Ian Pollock, a mind coach, in some weird old farmhouse in North Yorkshire. As I worked through the meditation course I began to realise I had lost sight of my dream.

However, meditation taught me to start visualising my dream again and problem solving. It gave me some 'tools', and during the winter John and I worked with them and had a really productive time. I was in a good frame of mind for the 1999 season that lay ahead, my first full year of motor racing.

It had been a long struggle and, at times, a miserable one up to this point, but now, with a good Mardi Gras drive lined up, I was doubly determined to succeed.

I treated it like a Formula One opportunity. I spent every minute of every day on that car. I worked on set-up with the mechanics, on my own performance, whatever it took to get ahead. I was eating and breathing with the team every day. We knew that if I wanted to become a professional driver I had to make a massive impact in 1999 and that meant winning races – nothing else would do.

The first race of the Renault Spider season was Donington Park. I visualised my first pole position and maiden race win – and I went out there and achieved both. It was all starting to come together.

All year I worked like a slave. I was so intense it really pissed off the team. At one point they even asked me to leave the outfit and run the car myself, albeit in a corner of the garage. I was constantly badgering the mechanics about things like checklists and set-up. I worked out that the 'flat patch' was not straight so demanded they sorted it. I was striving for absolute perfection. These guys were a professional team and engineering a great car, but were used to dealing with people who were racing for fun whereas this was the first step on the way to achieving my professional goals.

I remember having a really heated discussion with the team one night. Martin Sharpe, the boss of the team, was an ex-motorcycle rider who had developed a heart condition following a bad accident. And he said to me: 'You just need to calm down, Andy. You're just pushing us too far and too hard.'

However, I just wanted success so much I could not be told. The next night Martin did not feel too well, walked into a hospital and dropped dead of a heart attack. I was really shaken up by that because of our tough meeting. We dedicated the next race to Martin and I won it from pole position. One valuable lesson I learned from that whole experience was that winning is the best way to get everyone on your side. At the beginning of the year the team hated me but by the end I am sure they all loved me.

In all that year, I took a clean sweep of thirteen race wins, beating Jason Plato's record of eight successive victories from 1996 along the way. To add icing on the cake, I started each race from pole position and earned eleven fastest race laps.

The success brought me some recognition even if it did not bring much money. I was named as the Autosport/BRDC Club Driver of the Year and won the BARC President's Cup for Outstanding Achievement. I also landed the Guernsey Ambassador of the Year accolade. It felt good. I believed I was finally on the way although there was still a long way to go. I sold my championship-winning Renault Spider to John Reed of SG Hambros and, with that deal, began a long sponsorship association with the company. However, there were disappointments and one came the day after the glittering Autosport Awards gala night at London's Grosvenor House Hotel. I was driving to see Paul Stewart Racing about a potential Formula Three drive for the 2000 season. My phone rang and it was the team's Bruce Jenkins who told me not to bother – I was not on their list. I had just won everything I could during the 1999 season yet they did not even want to see me.

I could easily have moved into touring cars at that point. I had already tested for the Renault Williams Touring Cars Team and had quite a few opportunities to drive in the prestigious British Touring Car Championship. And I would have been paid, too. That would have been great for Jo because she could have gone out and bought some clothes! I was still living on £20 a week – that was the budget that Jo gave me. So I felt it was a huge decision to turn down a touring car drive and scrape by for another year. But, as ever, we managed to find a way.

I had to make some big decisions that winter about what I was going to do. I was handed a test in the Williams-Renault touring car, but managed to convince Tim Jackson, the boss of Renault UK, to give me a test in the team's Formula Three car instead. Nobody could really understand why I wanted to return to Formula Three, but I believed it was the 'Upper Sixth' of motor racing and I wanted to be seen as a world-class driver. I could have taken the easy route and been paid to drive in the British Touring Car Championship, but I wanted to look more long-term and do what was best for my career. Besides I was thinking that Formula One was still a possibility – and touring cars would not be the right route to the Grand Prix grid.

Anyway, I was given the test in Renault's Promatecme Formula Three car around Silverstone's short national circuit. At that time, I did not know how I was going to find the £250,000 required for the forthcoming season – but somehow I did. I turned up and met Serge Saulnier, the team boss. Promatecme had previously engineered current Honda Formula One ace Jenson Button in Formula Three so they knew what they were about and they said: 'Ah, we've got the Renault Spider Champion here. This is going to be funny …'

I had ten laps to prove I could drive to the level they wanted. I had prepared for that test as if it was for Formula One and I was so ready for it. In fact, the stop-watch showed that my lap times were very similar to Jenson's around the national circuit and following the test the team offered me the opportunity of a full day's testing at Magny-Cours in France.

However, when I arrived at Magny-Cours it was pouring with rain. I came out of the pits and promptly threw the car straight off the circuit. Magny-Cours is a really slippery track in the wet, but it was still embarrassing to have to return to the pits while the mechanics removed all the gravel from the car.

Luckily I was given another ten laps – and duly careered straight off through the gravel trap again! I came in and Serge pulled me to one side. 'Andy, we want you to go home,' he said. 'We're seeing exactly what we don't want to see.'

It was terrible and felt like the end of the world to me. I was thinking: 'I have put my whole life into this. Serge has given me a chance and I keep chucking it into the gravel.' But I refused to accept that it was over. I pleaded with Serge to give me one more chance. 'I promise I will show you what I can do,' I insisted. 'I'm sorry. I made mistakes, I was trying too hard. Just let me finish the day. I promise I won't let you down.'

He did not know what to say. He was probably worried about what I was going to do next and concerned his car might not make it through the day. Fortunately, he did give me another chance – and that was probably one of the most high pressure points in my career up to that time. Not only did I have to make sure I stayed on the track but I also had to prove my speed. I had to force the issue. Despite the pressure, I managed to prove my speed, did not put a wheel wrong and my lap times progressively came down.

After the test we went to the workshop and Serge said he would get back to me in a few days' time. He insisted the team had been really happy with my performance in the afternoon and the lap times were very quick. But, just when I was starting to feel better about everything, the big question landed: 'Oh, do you have the money?'

'Oh yes, I have the money,' I replied, 'but you know ...' Realistically, I did not have anything like the amount of money I needed. All I had was an opportunity to do touring cars, but I explained to Serge that I really wanted to do Formula Three and told him I had some sponsors that would help me with the funding. When we got home after the test I sat down with John Pratt to scribble ideas in my notebook.

We realised the size of the task ahead of us. To raise the quarter of a million pounds needed we had to source some serious backers. So we started the ball rolling there and then. A couple of weeks later the phone rang. It was Serge: 'Andy, we have decided we would like to have you in the team.'

I could have screamed at the top of my voice and it nearly brought a tear to my eye. Somehow I managed to stay relatively composed and responded: 'That's great news – what do we do next?'

'I send you the contract, you sign it and we start out testing,' he told me. 'We announce everything at the Autosport Show.' The annual Autosport motorsports show at the National Exhibition Centre in Birmingham was only a week away, in early January 2000. That was how fast things moved. I rang up Jo and yelled excitedly down the phone: 'I've got the Renault drive, the Formula Three Renault drive!'

The contract arrived and I had to find the required £250,000 personal liability. I signed the contract and then set about finding the money. My first port of call was the British Racing Drivers' Club at Silverstone. Having won every Renault Spider race the previous season, I had convinced the organisation of my ability so it agreed to give me a sum of money – which, coincidentally, was the exact amount of the first payment.

However, I had to chase the BRDC like hell to get the money quickly because Serge was chasing me for prompt payment of the first instalment. At that time I had generated some interest because of my all-conquering season in the Spiders. So a few sponsors were knocking around and, aside from the BRDC, SG Hambros had agreed to put in some funding.

I weighed it all up and believed I had something like 100 grand if all the proposed deals came together. I had some other long-shot sponsors; I was phoning people every day and doing proposals. However, once I received the money to cover the first payment it meant I could start testing, which was great.

I remember the official announcement at the Autosport Show. I was wheeled out in my big yellow Renault shirt with Matt Davies as my team-mate. Matt was seen by many as the next Jenson Button. The season before he had fought with Jenson and the championship winner Marc Hynes for podiums, so he was a well-rated driver.

However, I think almost everybody in motorsport was shocked I got the drive because I was viewed as little more than a good club driver. But I didn't care. I was by now 26 years old and not getting any younger ...

Anyhow, there I was in Formula Three with £250,000 to find and the first payment made. I found the money as best as I could throughout the year, and although I had a £40,000 shortfall at the end of the season, I had performed well enough to retain my drive. I was the rookie yet all year I outqualified and outraced Matt who should have been showing me the way. I had podiums but no wins because, as Sod's Law would have it, 2000 was the year the Renault engine was really bad.

I remember Bruce Jenkins, the team manager at Paul Stewart Racing, said: 'What's that fat old b*stard doing in Formula Three?' My first race in the 2000 season was at Thruxton and I qualified third. I think Bruce stopped talking about me in that way after that. All year I battled with the likes of Indian driver Narain Karthikeyan and Japan's Takuma Sato, both decent 'name' drivers who had spent a long time establishing their reputations and would eventually drive in Formula One. It had been tough but I had managed to complete my first full season of Formula Three.

At the end of the season I flew to Macau where I replaced Antonio Pizzonia who had won that season's British Formula Three title for Manor Motorsport. I had a really good weekend in Macau but unfortunately the team fuelled me short in qualifying, preventing me from earning what would probably have been a top-six place in qualifying. So I started from twelfth on the grid.

I really craved that Manor drive for the following season's British Formula Three campaign, picking up from where Pizzonia had left off. That team's Dallara-Honda was on another planet compared to the competition at the time. I knew I was in contention for the drive.

I also tested for the team that had just changed its name from Paul Stewart Racing to Jaguar. It had about eight drivers in contention for its race seats including James Courtney, Gary Paffett and Andre Lotterer. I was well in the mix and needed the drive – particularly because Jo and I still didn't have any real money behind us.

The Jaguar test was held at Oulton Park in Cheshire not long after I came back from Macau. I was hands down the quickest driver. I knew Paffett was good, he came from a world-class karting background and was highly rated, but I was one second a lap quicker than him during the test.

Alan Woodhead, my engineer who has worked with some great drivers such as current Honda Formula One star Rubens Barrichello, said to me: 'You've done a fantastic test, Andy. The feedback was good and you were fast. It is going to be my recommendation that the team hires you as the number-one driver and we have a younger man learning from you during the year.'

I could not believe it. I thought I had the Manor drive sewn up and now Jaguar were keen on me. It was Christmas and I had enjoyed a great season all told. I was on cloud nine.

Jo was heavily pregnant with Sebastian at this time so I really needed one of these race seats to give my career some proper momentum. As December wore on I heard nothing from Manor or Jaguar so began to chase things up. But all I heard was: 'Yes, yes, it is all good – we are still really interested, but still have not made our decision.' Considering we should have been starting testing in January, I was on a knife-edge.

Then, quite suddenly, everything went 'pear-shaped' just before Christmas when both the Jaguar and Manor drives fell through within a week.

Jaguar said: 'You are really great, but we are sorry ... we're going with Courtney and Lotterer.' I was stunned. These guys were nowhere near on my pace. Courtney had a great manager in Alan Gow who was well in with Jaguar and Lotterer was apparently related to a top-level guy at Jaguar's parent, Ford, so that was that. They were solid drivers but not at my level.

Later I learned the Manor deal fell through because a Northern Irish driver called Derek Hayes had subsequently come in with a very good offer. However, team boss John Booth had simply told me: 'It is just a gut feeling, Andy ...'

A gut feeling? In my mind, I knew exactly why Manor had hired Hayes over me ... I felt John was concerned about my funds and may have known I had struggled to meet all my payments in the past, although he would not say as much.

It was very hard to recover from that double-blow. We had little money and Seb, our first child, was due to arrive in six weeks' time. Once again, Christmas turned out to be tough. Everybody came out to visit us and we tried to have fun but I was devastated. After all my hard work and a truly brilliant season, we had nothing.

9 MAKING A NAME FOR MYSELF

> '<br>'I may have been a fast, committed and international-class driver, winning races with only the basic resources, but I did not have the correct media profile, or the back-up PR team, to promote myself properly.'

WHAT NEXT? After that dismal Christmas of 2000, I was pretty much at rock bottom. Just when I needed to be flying high I was scraping around looking for a drive again. I was by now 27 years old and not getting any younger, and I can assure you that, when it comes to finding a job, there is nothing like expecting a baby to put the pressure on. Serge Saulnier phoned me early in January 2001 and said Promatecme would like to have me back in its team for the forthcoming British Formula Three Championship title assault.

I was not thrilled. Even with only a few lukewarm irons in the fire it was not an attractive choice. After his initial phone call Serge had backed out completely and gone back to France having sold his share in the team to a new owner. And Renault had decided not to pump in any more money – basically, the French giant had pulled the plug. So the Renault engine was certainly not the way to go that coming season. All the other teams would be using Mugen-Honda powerplants ...

So I was unsure. Promatecme was a great team but it now felt a bit unstable. Looking back, I had joined the team as it was heading into a downwards spiral. Jenson Button had been there the year before me and had finished third in the championship, which was probably the peak for the team. But I kept talking to Renault over the winter and was also in contact with Alan Docking Racing. As usual, I did not have any money but was pushing my sponsors hard while trying to prepare for another season.

Then, out of the blue, we had a huge shock.

On 17 January, Jo and I went on one of those ante-natal classes where your partner is taught to breathe properly and so on. Poor Jo looked puffy and quite unwell, and did not really want to attend. I wanted to help her, though, so managed to persuade her that we should go. However, at the end of the class I asked the nurse to take a look at her.

Jo's blood pressure was alarmingly high – and the nurse said it would be best for her to visit hospital immediately. When we got to Northampton General we found out that the baby's heart rate was sky high as well. The medical staff carried out some tests and one of the team exclaimed: 'Oh, he is tiny, isn't he!' Jo had been undergoing regular check-ups and tests, and we had no indication at all that anything was wrong. So it came as a huge shock to be told the new baby was very small and would have to be delivered as soon as possible. Indeed, the hospital staff would have delivered him that night, but Jo had eaten a Mars bar so they could not operate. However, they kept a close eye on her all night, and I went home to Towcester absolutely devastated by the news and worried sick thinking of all the possibilities.

The next day, through emergency caesarean section, Sebastian was delivered. Although we had been warned the day before it was still a shock to see him. He was tiny and bright red. The umbilical cord had wrapped around his neck and he came very close to dying. Another day or so and he would have been gone.

I held this little man in my arms and I was overwhelmed with emotion. I thought to myself: 'I'm a failure. I have failed at racing – no team wants me. And now I've got to feed you. How am I going to do that?'

Seb was seriously ill for three weeks. He was fitted with tubes and we had to feed him one millilitre of milk every hour. But he did not take his feeds well and those three weeks were really difficult for everyone. Jo was ill and had also been very close to dying. I would go into Jo's room to check on her and then see how Seb was faring before making my calls about Formula Three in the parents' room. It was a desperate situation. I was worried sick yet having to keep my emotions under control while trying to work out some kind of future for the three of us.

At that time I was talking to Alan Docking Racing and several other teams. I did not want to give up on Formula Three but was struggling. A few sponsors came on board while Seb was really sick. Even at such a tough time, I had to keep strongly pushing for deals. And, in the end, I managed to scrape together enough money to sign with Alan Docking for 2001.

In one way, having this sense of purpose helped me retain some balance and perspective on life. I looked at what was really important to me. My child needed me to help him survive and I knew the only way was to be a successful dad. It made me even more focused and determined to make things happen.

Alan Docking Racing was a team that had not enjoyed much success for a long time, not since the days of Australian Mark Webber, the current Red Bull Racing Formula One driver who had been the last guy to win a race for them back in 1997. I went to the Silverstone-based team as the number-one driver, the man who was going to bring back some performance to it. With that in mind they agreed a deal at a lower rate, although I still had to find £200,000 rather than £350,000 for the season.

That year, incidentally, I used a caravan because I could not afford to stay in hotels with Seb needing so much medical care. I would be racing against Carlin Motorsport's Takuma Sato who, like Webber, went on to drive in Formula One, and quite a few other well funded, big-name guys. They had their posh motorhomes at the track and went off to stay in a big hotel during the evening while Jo and I lived with Seb – who was fighting for his life – in a caravan in order to save money to pay for our little son's medical care.

In that situation, Formula Three became a huge financial risk and the car was not even very good. I had only ten tests over the whole year while Sato had five times as many. He was razor-sharp yet I managed to have an amazing season.

I won at Snetterton, my first Formula Three race win, and thereafter managed to produce wins and podiums pretty consistently. Seb was only a few months old at the time of that Snetterton race and I still have the pictures of me holding him there – he had a knitted hat with the same design as my helmet. He was so tiny and looked sick. I fought all season, not quite for the championship but usually for a podium finish.

I was racing against, and beating, Courtney and Lotterer, the guys who 'replaced' me at Jaguar, in a car that was probably half a second slower than theirs. However, towards the end of the year we found some really good set-up combinations and I became increasingly competitive.

I scored ten podiums that season against the likes of Sato, Anthony Davidson – who also went on to Formula One – Courtney and Lotterer. And those guys were on big budgets in good cars that could win. In the end I finished sixth in the championship in a car that was little better than a B-class contender. It was a stunning season.

I wanted to end the season on a real high note so did a deal to return to Promatecme for the year-ending international events in Macau and Korea. Promatecme had always been a good team and now it had secured some decent Honda engines I was hopeful of scoring some good results.

The Macau Grand Prix is Formula Three's blue riband event and a win there pretty much guarantees the victor a seat in Formula One. I spent the first practice session just getting used to the car as I had not done much testing. I was banging my elbows, the gear-change was not right for me and the seat was uncomfortable.

As a result, I qualified only sixth quickest but in race one I got up to fourth pretty quickly. Then Derek Hayes, the guy that Manor had chosen over me thanks to team boss John Booth's 'gut feeling', launched himself over everybody and we had to have a restart. I had, by the way, outqualified him …

At the restart, I had a coming-together with another driver, clipped the barrier and was out of the running. I actually finished the race after we put the car back together, but I was never in with a chance. It was a real shame.

In race two, I came through the field right from the back to finish fifth. Last to fifth on a street circuit where it's extremely difficult to overtake – and passing guys who had been chosen for the better drives instead of me – was a good effort. I should have had a podium, and had the speed for sure, but touched the wall on the exit of the last corner.

From Macau I went to Korea for the Korea Super Prix and put the car straight on provisional pole. In the end, I qualified second to Jonathan Cochet, a good up-and-coming French driver, who had been quicker in his group session than I'd been in mine. In the race I was unable to pass Cochet and finished second. It was all I could do but still another very strong result. Given the strong competition, I was pretty pleased.

Heikki Kovalainen, the Finn who went on to drive for Renault and McLaren in Formula One, had also been among the field along with the guys I had been racing in the British Championship all year. And it was nice to go to Korea and absolutely blow away Derek Hayes. He had crashed a few times during the season so, despite putting together a half-decent season in the domestic championship, the 'gut feeling' that had earned him his place ahead of me proved somewhat unreliable in the end.

The prize money I earned was just enough to pay the team for the two drives and I left Korea as the best-placed Brit and one of the best international Formula Three drivers.

I beat six, seven or eight Formula Three champions, some of whom went on to race in Formula One, so was up there among the very best. But, if I am honest, I came home feeling a bit flat – I had given it my best shot but felt it was still not happening for me.

There had been no stone left unturned at that time. If there had been five quid of sponsorship money up for grabs I would have attempted to get it. I picked up every bit of financial backing I could, bolted all my deals together and, at the end of the day, drove two great seasons in Formula Three.

It took me from being a clubby to an international driver and, what's more, I managed to do it on my own along with the help of sponsors and my family. To complete two years in Formula Three, and raise all that money, was, I felt, pretty incredible.

I was still trying to push my career forwards, but although I was talking to some of the Formula One teams, like Prost and Jordan, I could not really see anything materialising from the discussions. They just wanted to know how much money I could bring, but I did not have the necessary marketing momentum behind me to makes things happen.

At that stage, I was struggling to get my name to the top of the Grand Prix teams' 'possibles' list because I was competing against drivers whose own media machines were constantly running. I was still relatively unknown. I went to Williams, for example, and was told: 'Andy, we have got a thick file on Jenson Button but hardly anything on you ...' I may have been a fast, committed and international-class driver, winning races with only the basic resources, but I did not have the correct media profile, or the back-up PR team, to promote myself properly.

It was not all doom and gloom. In my adversity, I found my versatility paid off ...

During that 2001 Formula Three season with Alan Docking Racing, I was offered a chance to race in a British Touring Car Championship event at Oulton Park. And, of all people, it was one of Jersey's best known residents I had to thank for that: Derek Warwick, a fellow Channel Islander and a good friend.

Derek phoned me out of the blue and asked what I was doing during the August bank holiday weekend – and would I fancy a drive in the forthcoming British Touring

Car Championship double-header at Oulton Park? It would be for Egg Sport, a Vauxhall satellite team. The team's regular driver, Phil Bennett, had been suspended so, obviously, I was more than happy to step in. Derek's Triple 8 Racing outfit was responsible for running four Vauxhalls, including the two Vauxhall Motorsport cars, entered that season.

I had raced at the Cheshire circuit during the Formula Three season but that would not be much help in touring cars. I had never tested this car, Astra Coupe, and, indeed, had never before raced in 'tin-tops'. I only had two free, thirty-minute practice sessions to get used to the car. In my first, remarkably, I posted the second-quickest time; however, in the second I put a wheel over the edge of a kerb, got a puncture and went straight into a tyre wall. It was a pretty bad crash so I sat out most of that session.

The car was looking pretty desperate for a time but the team managed to fix it. Derek had pushed me quite a lot for the drive so I do not think he wanted to show too much direct involvement with me at the meeting. He switched from being my friend, and a guy trying to help me, to behaving like a team owner, although it was done in the nicest possible way. Derek was a little disappointed I had fired off into the tyre wall but, at the same time, realised it was because of a puncture and, anyway, I was a rookie. And I had been quick. If I'd been slow that would have been a problem.

Then it was straight into qualifying. James Thompson was my Egg Sport team-mate, with Yvan Muller and Jason Plato in the Vauxhall Motorsport cars. These were good guys, experienced touring car winners – yet I just went out in my patched up car and stuck it on pole for both races.

After qualifying, everybody was clearly quite shocked, but nobody said too much because my car was 40 kg lighter than Muller and Plato thanks to the ballast penalties working in my favour. I was actually four-tenths of a second a lap faster in qualifying so, in my mind, I had worked out that I was a fair bit quicker than they were anyway. I played along with the 'obviously I am carrying no weight' line, but I still felt pretty special.

For me, I can safely say that performance started the touring car roller-coaster in motion and set the tone for my career to come …

In the first race, which was my first standing start in a front-wheel drive car, I spun the wheels too much, was overtaken by Yvan and finished second having tagged on to his rear bumper the whole race. I was close enough to overtake, but I was never really going to risk trying because I had crashed the car the day before and, anyway, Yvan was fighting for the championship.

Of course, I really wanted to make up for that and win the second race. I managed to make a good start and led for quite a while before Plato passed me. Then I became really involved in the action. Yvan tried to pass me but spun out on the grass. I tagged on to Plato's rear and was looking strong and about to overtake him when, unfortunately, my engine sump got damaged and I dropped oil everywhere. That was it.

But I knew I had showed good speed. I had notched two poles and a podium in my first British Touring Car Championship weekend. I left Oulton Park feeling that there was not much more I could do to secure a top drive so I just carried on with my normal Formula Three season, focused on trying to finish the year on a high with some more wins.

I think I was caught by surprise, however, by the interest that performance at Oulton Park stimulated. After months of near silence, it now seemed as if my phone was ringing all the time. For 2002 Vauxhall and Honda offered me a deal. Honda was worth £15,000 more, but with personal sponsors I could add another £50,000 if I did some more deals.

At the end of that Formula Three season I had been willing to consider any option. I was established in the category and winning races, but still did not know where the next buck was coming from.

And because I'd had such a bad time with very little money, I felt like some kind of tart, prostituting myself for money to simply go racing and live off other people's egos. I had never been very good at school, but when it came to doing deals and pushing things I could multi-task quite well. So I was just hustling my way through and hoping.

I did talk my way into a few Formula One test drives and felt I proved my speed when I did get on the track. I was in contact with the Prost Formula One team, and because I was sponsored by SG Hambros I was trying to broker a deal whereby we would put Prost sponsors' money into the banking firm and the resulting commission would help buy me a Formula One seat. That plan actually looked promising for a while. At the time I believed that I was a world-class driver but did not know how far that would take me. In hindsight, I probably could have made it to Formula One had I remained more of a dreamer and been a bit less sensible.

It was also a matter of age. Had I been a few years younger I would probably have made it to Formula One. But I started late and struggled, and that ultimately meant I missed the opportunity. And, as I've said before, I did not have the marketing behind me in Formula Three – I must have seemed anonymous for such a long time. My granddad, Skip, always said to me: 'If you want to sell a balloon, blow it up' and he was right. The problem was that I did not do that; I was waving around a deflated balloon.

I believe that in situations like the one I was in with Formula One, you have to read the signs and react. I am an intuitive dealmaker and could see possible chances with both Prost and Jordan, but there was nothing concrete in the offing because, quite frankly, my 2001 Formula Three season had not really been successful enough. I had not won sufficient races.

People were not shouting about me. They knew that I was quick but did not realise how little testing I'd had during the season. Sometimes I beat Takuma Sato but it was 'Sato comes second – oh, by the way, Priaulx won on a rain-swept track' – when I had shown great car control in the wet. Perhaps I didn't always get the credit I deserved.

So, once I'd weighed up all the options, I said to myself: 'What is really on the table here?' I had two touring car deals on the table that meant I would definitely be paid. And I had a potential deal in Formula One, but one that would require almost out of control levels of sponsorship. I had to choose between Vauxhall, Honda or Prost.

I had always told Jo that by the time I had reached 30 I wanted to be a fully professional racing driver. So, there I was heading towards my 28th birthday with an opportunity to be paid and earnings higher than ever before. I realised that Formula One probably would not happen and, to be honest, I would have had to go through another year of finding £300,000, £400,000, £500,000 or maybe

£1 million just to have a good Formula Three season. So I took the Honda deal – and have never looked back ...

After the years of struggle, the Honda deal was a big thing for Jo and I. We were living in Towcester and had big debts built up over various seasons of racing. I had a duty to provide for my family and now had a decent opportunity to do so. It was not a lot of money but it was a start and I worked out very quickly that if I could keep some of my personal sponsors I would then make more money.

However, I remember thinking there was a fair bit of a risk in agreeing the deal. When I agreed to drive for Honda Racing UK, whose campaign was run by Arena Motor Sport, the team was still to tie up all the final details with Honda. Motor racing is full of promises, half-deals, agreements that are not completed and dreams that are not realised. It is not the fault of the people involved because, often, there are so many outside influences complicating the situation. Still, I had signed up and kept my fingers crossed everything would work out for 2002 – which, in the end, it did.

I have seen talented people like Matt Davies, from Formula Three, come and go yet I am still here. I have met some amazing drivers in my career and I have transformed myself from living in a caravan with no money to realising my dream of becoming a fully paid professional driver at the highest level outside of Formula One.

I do not think it gets much better than that. The Formula One dream had been there for a while but I learned that Grand Prix racing is not just about talent. It is also about money and politics. I made it to Formula Three but Formula One did not happen, yet I gave it my best shot and left no stone unturned in my efforts.

My decision to secure the future and face a new challenge in the British Touring Car Championship was the best one I could make at that time. And to go from racing motocross on the sand in Guernsey to becoming a three-time world champion is a very satisfying achievement. I know that the decisions I made in 2001, when I had many different options, were pivotal in that journey.

10 EARNING A LIVING

'Everyone in Britain said I was mad to drive in the European Touring Car Championship. I heard it all: "All the best touring car drivers are in Europe" … and even "You are going to fail and come back with your tail between your legs."'

I DID MY HONDA TOURING CARS DEAL with a guy called Mike Earle. Mike is a good friend of Bernie Ecclestone, the Formula One commercial rights-holder, and knows his way around the British and international motor racing scene. He runs Arena Motor Sport, the team that would receive Honda's full factory backing for the forthcoming 2002 British Touring Car Championship season and compete under the Honda Racing UK banner.

After his help the previous year in giving me my first British touring cars chance, I felt really bad not signing with Derek Warwick at Vauxhall. In all honesty, I stood to earn a lot more money by going to Honda. Derek had told me that money should not be so important and, in many respects, he was right. But I felt it was an easy thing for him to say when he earned a shed load of money from his Formula One career with the likes of Renault, Lotus and Footwork. For me, the situation was entirely different.

I had to do the best deal for me and to help secure the future of my family. I knew I was taking a big gamble going to a new team, with a car that had never been tested. And I had only the briefest of touring car experience at that point. But, I must say, my first season with Honda was, ultimately, very successful.

I should have expected it even though it was still a tough learning experience. The first half of the year was terrible. The Civic Type-R would not even steer in a straight line without trying to spin out of my hands. It had terrible torque steer yet was fast with a strong engine and, under-neath, was a decent machine. I kept my spirits up by thinking about the deal, of Seb and Jo, and all the good reasons for pressing on at that time.

My team-mate was an Irishman called Alan Morrison, a really sound guy and a very quick driver. He was actually more of a motocross superstar than a racing driver, but he had natural speed and – a big advantage over me, this – more front-wheel drive experience. I had come straight from single-seaters, bar that one-off British Touring Car Championship race meeting at Oulton Park the previous year. So, as expected, the first half of the season was a series of learning experiences for everyone, problems to be overcome and a gradual improvement in package and performance.

However, by mid-season, we had managed to sort out the problems and things began to fall into place. Things improved all the time, and by the end of the year I was one of the main contenders having won one race and finished on the podium on two other occasions to claim fifth overall in the championship. I never actually had a chance to win the title but was the highest points scorer in the second half of the season – and I won Honda's first race under the new regulations. That race win, which delighted us all so much, came at Knockhill in Scotland. It was a pretty special and remarkable achievement all told.

One of the reasons for that success, and why I believed I did so well in my first full touring car season, was the link I established with 1991 British Touring Car Champion, the late Will Hoy. I did a deal with Will that saw him attend my races as an engineer-cum-mentor. I felt it might be useful to draw on his experience and knowledge – and it was. Will was able to pass on a lot of very astute advice and guidance for which I was extremely grateful.

I was deeply shocked during that season when I found out he had a brain tumour. I first noticed it when we were talking on the car radio and he began missing a few lines which I thought was strange. The following weekend I phoned him and it was another difficult conversation.

I asked Will if he was okay. 'Oh, yeah, you know, just a few headaches and whatever,' he assured me. 'I'm going to the doctor about it – it isn't a problem. Don't worry.' Soon after that conversation we all learned he had a serious brain tumour and sadly died within three months in December 2002.

So, fresh from having had a brilliant debut season with Honda, I was having to deal with another big shock. It seemed as if things were destined never to run smoothly for long.

Having done so well, establishing both myself and the team, I felt confident I would have a good chance in 2003 to win the championship. So I went to see Mike Earle when the season was over to renegotiate my existing two-year contract.

I was due a rise under the terms of the initial deal, but I felt I was now worth a bit more and did not expect Honda to disagree. But when I confronted Mike with my request, I was horrified to find out that Honda had completely pulled the plug. What Mike actually said was: 'Well, actually, Andy, we are not going to pay you anything because we don't have a contract anymore … We want you to drive for us, but we cannot pay you.'

That winter I negotiated a deal to drive in the classic Bathurst 1000 for 2003. I remember the occasion well because it happened in the middle of the night. My phone rang and it was BMW – well, not actually BMW but an agent called Ian Flux.

'Andy, Andy,' he exclaimed. 'I have negotiated a deal for you, but before I tell you who it is I want you to sign this contract and fill me in for ten per cent.' Obviously I found out more about the deal to reassure myself before replying: 'Right, just send me the contract and I will sign it.' At that time I was down in Australia to do the classic Bathurst 1000 and Queensland 500 enduros with the HRT Holden Kmart Racing team. But I had no permanent deal for 2003 and so was not in any position to be too choosy.

I discovered that BMW had actually said they wanted me for their 2003 European Touring Car Championship campaign after just a single season in the British Touring Car Championship, so I did not actually need to go through Fluxie at all. They would have got me anyway.

The deal cost me some money, but Ian had been sharp and you have to take your hat off to him for that! And at least things were on the up again.

I did the Bathurst 1000, alongside Yvan Muller, my old Vauxhall colleague from 2001, but the race turned out to be a bit of an anti-climax when the car blew up at halfway.

As I travelled home to complete that BMW deal, I felt really excited although still not certain whether it would actually happen. I saw Peter Walker, my boss at BMW UK, who told me: 'We've got driver A, driver B and driver C on our list. What sort of money would you like?'

I thought about it and pitched myself at a price that, at the time, was quite well paid for a driver like myself who had proved he could do well but was not yet a champion. I knew the other guys would ask for a bit less but I went for it anyway. At the end of the meeting, Peter said: 'Well, we are interested, and we'll get back to you ...'

That was a massively important moment for me. It was a situation in which where I'd had to draw on all my negotiating experience gathered from being, at various times, a crazed sponsorship chaser, used car salesman, natural dealmaker and gritty survivor. I just knew deep inside that sometimes you cannot leave a deal open and let the person you are talking to phone you back later. In my car salesman days I learned that if somebody walked out of the showroom without a deal, they would more than likely see something else. I figured the same principle applied with BMW.

My attitude was to do the deal there and then. So I said: 'Listen, Peter, that was the price for the deal. Whether or not you want to do a deal, I have Honda ready to sign me. Are we going to do it or not?' And straightaway he responded: 'Yep – deal.' It was the start of my BMW career.

I spoke afterwards to former BMW ace Steve Soper and found that he had actually recommended me for the seat having seen my performances with Vauxhall. Steve assured me I had done the right thing in the negotiations because they always believed the last person they had spoken to.

However, everyone in Britain said I was mad to drive in the European Touring Car Championship. I heard it all: 'Nobody is going to respect you' ... 'All the best touring car drivers are in Europe' ... 'You do not know any of the circuits' ... 'You are a one-car team' ... and even 'You are going to fail and come back to BTCC with your tail between your legs.'

Fair comment. It could end up that way. But I was going to try it anyway. I had my first test at Monza soon after Peter had signed me and that went really well. I showed some good speed and the team liked the way I worked. Afterwards I returned to the UK and enjoyed a long break from November to February with no driving while the team put everything together for the forthcoming 2003 season.

Then I had a phone call to go to Monza.

Monza is famous as the most pure and historic Grand Prix venue in Italy. But I had never before been to the great old circuit situated in the former royal parkland, half an hour north of Milan. I knew of its reputation and history, of course, but not the details of the track, each change of camber, the bumps and, most importantly, the chicanes. It is a low downforce, high-speed track with a lot of trees close by.

I had ten laps in the BMW works car, run by the hugely respected Schnitzer team, to prove myself. I saw it as an opportunity to learn the circuit and get some miles in before the season started. I had to wait ages for my chance and then, half an hour before the end of the day, it came at last. I jumped in and after a quick seat fitting – and the seat still did not feel right when I went out – the team said: 'Okay, you have ten laps.' I had heard that sentence somewhere before and old memories of my Renault Formula Three test reverberated in my mind …

What I did not realise at the time was that Schnitzer would be one of the main rivals I was going to be racing against in the season as BMW Team Germany. I had just thought, perhaps naively: 'We are a BMW team, so are they, and they will look after me …' Well, er, no, not quite, Andy. It may have been a BMW team but this was a competition in which I was a rival and had to be beaten – well beaten if possible.

I had ten terrible laps. I spun the car, over-revved it and ended up in the gravel. I duly had the same conversation with Schnitzer boss Charly Lamm afterwards that I had once had with Serge Saulnier at Promatecme. 'Look, I'm really sorry,' I said. 'I'm just pushing too hard. Give me another chance. I'll get my act together.'

I did not get another chance.

I found out later that BMW had then tried to replace me after that Schnitzer test because the powers-that-be had not liked what they had seen – and who could blame them! But my team, BMW UK, stood up for me, claiming I had performed well in its tests and deserved another go. So I started off on the back foot once again.

I knew I had to prove myself, and quickly. If I did not my days were numbered. I also knew that from then until the end of my contract I would have them watching me. I had just one test booked before the season was due to open in Valencia in Spain.

The test was held at the Circuit de Catalunya, near Barcelona. And I was not actually that quick so the BMW UK team was understandably starting to get worried. I remember the conversations well: 'Andy, we're not seeing it. You are two seconds off the pace of Dirk Muller (one of the Schnitzer drivers). He is up there and you are down here. Why is that?' They started to question my driving.

I said to my team boss, Bart Mampaey: 'Look, you signed me, now stick with me. I am going to prove you have made the right decision, but you need to give me the car with the speed and it will work for me.'

Fortunately, Bart was understanding and told BMW GB: 'Listen, guys, he's going to need some more tests before the first race otherwise he's not going to be up to speed.'

Peter Walker and Chris Willows from BMW GB were great. They agreed to provide more money for further tests, and by doing that demonstrated they would stick by me.

I badly needed this support at that time. We carried out five or six more tests and I found a setting on the car I really liked and which suited my driving style. The final pre-season test was at Spa-Francorchamps, one of the great old-style European race circuits that runs out around a valley filled with pine trees in the Belgian Ardennes forest.

Team Germany was also there in Belgium and, to show the doubters what I was made of, I just went quicker and quicker. Spa has always been regarded as a circuit that 'separates the men from the boys' and my performance was absolutely what I needed. In the last hour of the test, I hit upon an optimum setting and blew away my rivals, including Dirk Muller. I had made my point.

We shipped the car to Barcelona and I was totally fired-up to show the Spa testing performance hadn't been a fluke and that I could reproduce it in a real race situation. I had done a full season of British touring cars the previous year and still had all my belief. Now was the time to prove my worth – and keep my job.

11 RACING INTO EUROPE

'It was a crazy move from Tavano. He took a
lunge at me on the brakes and fired me off.
I was furious. I had been quite cool until
that point, but when I later walked
past the Alfa Romeo garage
I just went crazy.'

WE FLEW OUT TO SPAIN. At last, I had the feeling that I
was doing what I really wanted to. I was now a paid,
respected international racing driver and travelling around
Europe to contest the 2003 European Touring Car Championship for BMW Team GB. I had a few butterflies in my
stomach and was still a bit unsure about certain things,
but for someone racing at that level for the first time, with
a team and car I was still getting to grips with, that was
understandable. After the pre-season test at Spa-Francorchamps, I felt I had found a good set-up and had the pace.
It was now just a case, or so it seemed, of making sure
nothing had been lost and repeating my best work from
Belgium.

We turned up at the Barcelona track and my BMW 320i
was pretty competitive straightaway in free practice. That

was to be expected. But I had prepared myself well and I was right in among them. Come qualifying I went out on new tyres and immediately put the car on the provisional front row. I had laid down a marker. However, as the session wore on, I slipped back quite a bit on the grid because the Alfas were so dominant, although BMW was pretty close behind. The Team Germany team went a bit quicker than me in qualifying as I battled to understand how to get the maximum out of both the car and the heated tyres.

But when the two races came around I was really competitive. I finished sixth in the first one behind the Alfa of Gabriele Tarquini, the great Italian driver previously in Formula One who was not only one of the best touring car 'peddlers' around but a good bloke to boot. He actually went on to win the championship that year.

In the second race, I improved to take third place. Team Germany scored a one-two, and I was right behind, actually trying to overtake. I recalled the famous Austrian former Formula One ace Gerhard Berger, who was working for BMW at the time, exclaiming: 'Who is this Priaulx guy?' They were stunned because no other BMW team had been anywhere near Schnitzer's pace until then.

Schnitzer had covered thousands of testing miles in the car so we would always be playing catch-up, especially at the beginning of the season. But we had always refused to accept that they could not be challenged and worked as hard as we could to demonstrate that.

To cut a long story short, I built up my confidence and knowledge during the first half of the season with several solid performances, showed off my speed a little bit and was then ready to start winning. I duly took my first victory in Brno, in the Czech Republic, and then in Spa-Francorchamps and then again in Oschersleben in Germany. Suddenly this rookie, who was almost replaced before the season started, found himself fighting for the championship crown going into the final double-header meeting at Monza in Italy.

I recalled one of the top guys at BMW, Dr Mario Theissen, who is in charge of all the motorsport and who runs the Formula One team, came to see me, at the start before the final race. As things had turned out, despite being a rookie, I was BMW's only hope of winning the championship.

He opened the door and said to me: 'We support you, you are our only chance.' I had made it and all eyes of BMW were upon me. There was still one race to go and Jörg Muller, of Schnitzer, did not have a mathematical chance to win, but I did – and in my rookie season. I was a threat and a fly in the ointment for a few people's plans.

I was not given much of a chance to show what I could do. Instead, my title challenge ended ingloriously when

I was taken out at the first corner of the final race by Alfa driver Tarquini, the champion, who shoved Duncan Huisman into the back of me and sent me into a spin. It was a hard pill to swallow and showed how tough the series could be. I was a British driver representing a BMW team in a scrap for a European title with an Italian driver in an Italian car and on Italian soil.

If that situation occurred now I would be really hacked off. Coming third in the championship would be a big downer for me. But then, I had just come from the British Touring Car Championship where I had won just one race and finished fifth in the 2002 series. So to finish third in a European championship, in a season in which I had to learn all the circuits, and score three victories with eight podium finishes and one pole position made it a very special year.

When I left British touring cars, people said I would be chewed up and spat out in the European series. But that was the first year I was properly recognised as a good international driver. At the end of the year, I watched the seasonal review on DVD and all the drivers, Tarquini and so on, whom I had looked up to for a long time were filmed saying how impressed they had been with my performance.

That gave me a lot of confidence. I had made my mark and, using my momentum built up from that season,

One of many
'pose for the
camera' shots:
Silverstone 1999.

John Pratt offers valuable advice back in Formula 3 days.

Who says it's not a contact sport?

I am honoured with my own postage stamp, Brands Hatch in 2006.

Laser vision. It's
in the eyes…

First corner disaster at Valencia in 2006. One of the perils of the rolling start –
poor old Huffy didn't make it the next couple of times either!

Above Three FIA World Champions: with Fernando Alonso (F1) and Sebastien Loeb (Rallycars), distinguished company in Monaco.

Right I am World Champion...fantastic!

My 'office'.

Above Mum said the choir, I said motorsport, Jo said X Factor?

Above A home win means everything…WTCC, Round 17, in 2007.

On the hallowed turf at Wembley during the Race of Champions. Great fun.

Above More PR at the Autosport International Show, Birmingham 2007, with Takuma Sato.

Above A very proud day as I receive the BRDC Gold Medal from Damon Hill.

Leading at Macau. No better feeling, with the 2007 World Championship just round the corner.

Above The 2008 WTCC, Brazil. Podiums are great, whichever step you are on. prefer the top one though.

The boys at RBM are my extended family. Thanks, guys, you're the best

One for the sponsors. Cheers, guys!

I negotiated a really good, improved, two-year contract with BMW. In every way, I was all set to start 2004 with a really good chance to win the title.

Incidentally, while 2003 had been a season full of hard racing, it was also one full of novelty and surprises for me – and because of that it was fun. After one test at Hockenheim, instead of driving straight to the next race at Brno in the Czech Republic, myself and Chris Cramer – a good friend and mentor who travels with me quite a lot – decided to take the train.

Unfortunately, instead of getting a comfortable and fast night-sleeper, this dilapidated and smelly old train rolls into the station. To make matters worse, we were woken in the middle of the night by a Czech guy in a uniform who came into our cabin waving his gun around and asking for our passports.

Normally a really gentle guy, this was just too much for Chris – a former British Hillclimb Champion – who got really grumpy. He turned to me with a face like thunder and said deadpan: 'B*gger me, that guy was born ugly!' Needless to say, when I told the team the next day they found the whole tale highly amusing!

Over the winter of 2003–04 I had been to Macau again, this time with BMW Motorsport run by Carly Motors, where

I finished runner-up in the first race after qualifying fourth but failed to finish the second. I also flew to Australia and raced once again for the Holden Kmart team, this time in the Sandown 500, in which I finished twelfth, and, as in 2002, the blue riband Bathurst 1000; sadly, I failed to start the latter because of a startline accident by my team-mate.

As if that was not enough, it was while I was in Macau that Danniella, our second child, was born five weeks premature. Jo was very poorly and I was on the other side of the world unable to do anything to help. I was just thankful she was being cared for at the Princess Elizabeth Hospital in Guernsey, and more thankful when both mother and daughter recovered completely.

Then, at the end of a year in which I had also been busy helping train the 'drivers of the future' in the new Formula BMW UK series, I won the BMW Sports Trophy for non-works BMW drivers.

The way in which I was involved in so many different things, yet managed to remain focused on my race-driving for BMW, helped me succeed in 2003, I am sure. I was always ready to improve myself and, with that kind of attitude, I was keen to get back into action when the new European season got underway at Monza.

This time the BMW 320i car was fast straightaway and I understood both it and the team much better by now. All the teams came out fighting, too. In my first pre-season test at Monza, the car showed its pace, and although not as fast as the Schnitzer cars I was not too worried. I knew that come the race weekend at the Italian circuit, I would be competitive. So I felt confident and positive.

My optimism was vindicated because, to cut a long story short, this time I started winning much earlier in the season. This brings me on to something that annoys me greatly: that with success comes penalty ballast ...

Having worked as hard as you can to put together the best package to succeed, you are then weighted down to prevent you from winning again. I do not like this regulation and cannot understand it, but I suppose it keeps the field level. The ballast was not my only problem. I began to feel like a marked man after a few successful races and people started to act quite cold with me. There was definitely a bit of tension between the teams in the pit lane and the atmosphere was pretty frosty at times.

Also – and I don't know if it had anything to do with it – I was now bringing my own motorhome to race meetings in order to not only have my family with me but my own private space.

Anyhow, as I'd hoped, I was quick that first race weekend at Monza. I never feel on real top form there because it is one of those circuits where you benefit from a team-mate pulling you along in his slipstream – and being a single car team meant I would have to rely on other cars doing me a favour …

I also felt a little more 'noticed' on the track, too. During the previous season nobody seemed to care if I followed them closely, but suddenly drivers were trying to make my life more difficult. If I latched onto someone before the start of a quick lap they would slow up or pull over and abort theirs, or just generally try and unsettle me. So I had to try a different tactic and simply be more opportunistic in qualifying.

I qualified sixth quickest and finished fifth in race one. Fortunately, I was able to benefit from the reverse grid for the second race and followed fellow BMW driver Jörg Muller home to take second place.

I had known Monza would be tough, with all the slipstreaming, so to score some solid points, including a podium finish, represented a decent return from the first weekend of the season. My more seasoned sense of judgement overcame my frustration at not being able to win.

The circus then moved to Valencia, a meeting that I remember very well for all the wrong reasons. I suffered from very bad food poisoning all weekend – indeed, I have seen some photos taken of me then and I was literally green. And my father picked it up as well. We both felt awful.

That race weekend was also when I first started to notice that my dad did not seem very well generally. Until that point, none of us realised he had Parkinson's disease, but when he went down with food poisoning it became pretty obvious. Whereas I managed to get through the weekend he, unfortunately, could not and had to stay in his hotel room the whole time.

Alfa was on another planet that weekend with Augusto Farfus qualifying on pole position. Gabriele Tarquini won the first race and team-mate Fabrizio Giovanardi took the second. I was carrying 25 kg of success ballast, as were the unrelated Schnitzer boys Dirk and Jörg Muller, yet still managed to net solid points following fourth and sixth place finishes – crucial in the overall championship picture. But the really positive thing was that I had been extremely quick in qualifying – half a second faster than the works cars.

I qualified fourth fastest. But I could not eat or drink, had aching bones and felt absolutely lousy. Luckily, it was close to the beginning of the season so it was not too hot, but I was still getting very dehydrated. I remember thinking: 'I'm a professional driver, I can't be sick at a race.' It can be quite a scary situation. If something like that happens, you either drag yourself into the car or potentially you might lose your job.

After the two free practice sessions I just lay in the truck hoping to feel better. When qualifying started I had to dig really deep to get in my lap and to end up half a second faster than the nearest BMW was, I felt, a truly excellent effort in the circumstances. I knew I was fit but it was sheer willpower and determination that got me through that meeting.

Luckily, I was still at that early stage in the European touring cars career where everything I did was looked upon with rose-tinted spectacles. It was similar to Lewis Hamilton's experience in the 2007 Formula One season when he was a rookie and finished second in the title race: if I did well it was great; if I did not it was obviously somebody else's fault because I was the underdog. A real no-lose situation ...

Magny-Cours next up was interesting for several reasons. It was the first meeting at which I had the motorhome – I thought having one would improve my race weekend performance and demonstrate to BMW my level of commitment. We had little Danniella with us for the first time – she had been born the previous November – and it was such fun as I drove down to the French circuit with the family on board. Seb, then three, was at the age when he was 'into everything' and Dannii was a little squawking baby. We felt like a proper family and it was a lovely feeling.

Having been sick at the last race meeting in Spain, this time it was poor Danniella's turn to suffer as she went down with chicken pox. We noticed one spot before we left home and by the time we got to Magny-Cours she was absolutely covered, had a high temperature and was really unwell. It was a very trying weekend.

We had to call a doctor out. Dannii, though strong when she was born, was a little bit sick as well. She was born premature and tended to pick up chest infections and coughs very easily, so this bout of chicken pox worried us. I was trying to race but it was not easy to concentrate in those circumstances. However, I managed to have a good weekend and won my first race of the year – a sign that I could perform even when there were distractions around me.

I suppose the benefits of the motorhome had begun to outweigh the disadvantages. For the first time I had been able to eat my normal English food at races and have a routine. I had felt sick for the whole of the previous season and seemed to pick up stomach problems almost every-where. Now, though, I had English tea and my own pasta, a poached egg each morning. I was no longer living a hospi-tality suite diet and feeling sick most of the time. My immune system had not built up sufficiently by that time and I was still unused to much travelling.

On the track that weekend I finished eighth in race one, so I benefited from the reverse grid system to start from pole in the second. While it was nice to be first on the grid I was very worried about the pace because Jörg and Dirk Muller were very, very quick. Anyway, worried or not, I managed to take my first race victory of the season and set the fastest lap to boot, giving the Priaulx clan cause for a happy trip home. It was just the result we wanted to boost my confidence after three of the season's ten meetings.

At Hockenheim for rounds seven and eight, my car was simply fantastic. Unbelievably quick. Starting third on the grid after qualifying I proved my pace was good enough to win by claiming the opening race honours. That was two wins on the spin following my success at Magny-Cours. I was on a roll.

Hockenheim is a good, fast circuit set in the forests south of Heidelberg, a beautiful university city in Germany. All the BMWs were quick there but I felt as if mine was faster than ever before. Being one of BMW's two 'home' races that season the crowd was a good size. Funnily, you never really notice that kind of thing when you are in the car itself. You feel so enclosed in the cockpit, and it's so hot and noisy with so much going on, you can hardly take in the crowd. You tend to notice it a lot more in *parc ferme* when you climb out of the car.

My confidence was high after that win. In race two I made a great start to fight my way through the field from eighth on the grid, on the way setting what would turn out to be the fastest race lap. I was hoping for a podium finish, and maybe even a win. As I made progress I had a decent battle with Antonio Garcia of BMW Spain and managed to overtake him with a great move under braking.

BMW, incidentally, has always been good about allowing its teams to scrap in a hard but fair way against each other. After all, the manufacturer feels that such a tactic can only drive up the whole level of performance.

Unfortunately, a stone holed the radiator so I had to pull over and retire after six laps. It was not my fault so I could not be too unhappy, but helped add to my feeling that I'd had a good start to the season.

That night something odd happened. I was asleep in the motorhome and was woken by some loud snoring so got up to investigate. It was neither Jo nor my father so I could not understand it. I went outside to take a look around and the perpetrator turned out to be some tramp who had crawled under the vehicle and was sleeping on the grass right under my bed. In the end, we had to usher him away, but even that disturbance could not dampen my spirits. I was feeling good.

The next double-header was Brno in the Czech Republic and, because my father was not feeling 100 per cent well, I decided to bring along a friend to help with the driving. While it was good to have, taking my motorhome to and from the races involved a lot of driving and, to be honest, I only did it for one year before paying for a driver. It was fun, though. Jo and I were young, the kids were not yet at school and it offered a chance to see Europe and travel around. It seemed like a real adventure at that time.

We witnessed all sorts of things, some dazzling and extraordinary, and some just plain awful. Driving through Brno, for example, I saw my first dead body after some guy had jumped off a bridge. With us were two friends: Andy Richmond, a motocross mate, who we imaginatively called 'Lizzie' because he looks like a lizard, and his girlfriend Carlee. We were all a bit shocked by what we'd seen but I was determined not to let it upset my weekend.

And the weekend was good. I qualified second and won the first race, which was excellent considering I was carrying extra weight ballast. I started from eighth on the grid in race two but still came home second behind Dirk Muller's similar BMW. I was not benefiting from the reverse grid system anymore and was being pushed back, a sign that I had real speed. I was by now qualifying strongly and winning races. I had become a serious title contender.

I had now triumphed at three successive meetings: Magny-Cours, Hockenheim and Brno. So, I was beginning to feel very proud of myself. Not for long, though ...

I had arranged a barbecue by the motorhome on the Sunday evening. My family was with me in this gorgeous forest setting and I had a glow of satisfaction because I felt I was now one of the best drivers in the series. Life could not be much better, I thought.

Unfortunately, I had contrived to leave the new barbecue at the checkout of the French supermarket at which we had bought it on our way to Brno. We had the table and chairs, and the meat, but no barbecue ... In the end, the girls did the cooking so we still had a lovely meal.

Following the Brno meeting – the halfway point in the championship race – I was at the sharp end of the standings which, as ever, meant I had to carry extra weight ballast. The next race was my home race in Britain, at Donington Park. I particularly wanted to do well there because the boss of BMW GB was not that keen on motor racing.

It may have been that I tried too hard to impress him, however, because I had a rotten qualifying session and sat thirteenth on the grid. The car was terrible in free practice and no better in qualifying. In fact, after struggling in the latter I had my first real argument with the team, which was a shame. There was a quite bit of pressure and the tension was palpable. The team looked over the car and found that a wishbone had not been running freely, which had really affected my performance. It just goes to show that you are only as strong as your weakest link in motor racing ...

We duly fixed the problem and I was encouragingly quick in the race warm-up. Once the first race got underway I managed to fight my way up to sixth with lots of overtaking to thrill my home crowd.

The reverse grid system worked in my favour for race two allowing me to start from third spot. I was still driving one of the heaviest cars, thanks to the penalty ballast, but I won comfortably. And when I drove back into the garage everyone was swilling champagne! That made it four meetings in a row at which I had won – and guess what? I was now leading the championship by four points with eight events remaining.

Donington had attracted a great crowd so it was fantastic to stand on the podium and absorb the excellent, and vociferous, support. The motor racing press were excellent, too. I had always thought the championship lacked a bit of national exposure, but I was enjoying some mainstream coverage now. Although it was nothing like it is now, and would be when I won the world titles, I did not care too much. I was getting paid and winning races – and I had just triumphed in my home race. I was flying.

Spa-Francorchamps in Belgium is another venue that has always been good for me. The previous year I took my maiden pole position there in front of Dr Mario Theissen, the BMW motorsport chief. This year, because of the success ballast, I did not really expect to be fighting for

pole. However, I qualified fourth, and finished the weekend with fourth and fifth places, which was fine.

I did not lose any championship points to my rivals so
it was a solid weekend overall. But when we went to Imola
in Italy, for rounds fifteen and sixteen, it was much less
straightforward. We had some major dramas with the car
so we tried some different dampers that only made the
handling worse. It was skipping and bouncing everywhere
so it was no surprise to be nearly last in practice.

That came as a shock because I was fighting for the
title and used to being at the front. However, we managed
to sort the car, putting back on the old dampers, and I
qualified ninth. Race one brought me a fifth place, so with
the reverse grid I started fourth for race two. But I could
not keep up my run of finishes because Salvatore Tavano's
Alfa had a coming-together with me on the fourth lap.

It was a crazy move from Tavano. He took a lunge at
me on the brakes and fired me off. I was furious. I had
been quite cool until that point, but when I later walked
past the Alfa Romeo garage I just went crazy; of course,
the television cameras picked it up and that incident was
used in the end-of-year review footage of the season.

Some people quite liked my 'strop', though. A few said:
'It was good to see a bit of fight from you, Andy'. I was
really disappointed with Alfa. I felt the shunt could have
been avoided and, because it was now getting towards the

business end of the season, I was more than suspicious about the motives. Alfa won everything at Imola – Gabriele Tarquini and Fabrizio Giovanardi finishing one-two in both races – and I remember seeing the three works Alfa drivers, including Augusto Farfus, on the podium after race one and feeling really sick.

The Autodromo Enzo e Dino Ferrari may be a beautiful circuit, set among the rolling vineyards of Emilia-Romagna, but Imola has, of course, seen a lot of incident and tragedy down the years and was, of course, the scene of the deaths in the 1994 San Marino Grand Prix of Roland Ratzenberger and three-time World Champion Ayrton Senna. My shunt annoyed me greatly, but it was just another footnote in the records of motorsport that are littered with similar happenings.

After spending the day after the race reflecting and recharging my batteries on the beach at Rimini – a 'Guernsey moment' – I was back on form at Oschersleben in Germany. I qualified second and won the opening race. Fantastic! I was back in the fight again. But in race two, after I'd picked my way through from eighth position, I came across another Alfa, Augusto Farfus this time, and he fired me off as well …

Yes, European touring cars is a contact sport. It's also highly political and this was the first season in which I learned to understand the real extent of that. The problem is I am not really a political guy. I just get in my car and try to race it to the limit and win. But, at that time, Alfa was fighting for the title as well and Tarquini's Alfa mates – perhaps only by coincidence – kept being involved in incidents with me. To make things worse Dirk Muller, my close rival for the title, had a great weekend in the Schnitzer BMW.

Muller took third and second places that meant I would be heading towards Dubai, for the final meeting of the year, well and truly on the back foot. I was really annoyed because, up to then, I had won more races – five – than anybody else. Race after race I had performed and now I was 12 points off the pace heading into the final two races.

Although I now felt the title was a long shot I was determined to haul it back within reach and teach everybody a lesson. I had been through so many tough times and was not about to give up easily.

This time, facing this challenge, I was comforted by the thought that I had a brilliant team behind me. My boss, Bart Mampaey, and my engineer Sam Waes were as determined to win as I was. I resolved to get as fit as possible to cope with the heat and humidity of Dubai, even working out in the gym in my racing suit.

I then headed off to Dubai. There, thanks to two second places – both behind Tarquini – I duly returned with the championship crown having ended the season tied on points with Dirk Muller and winning out courtesy of five wins to three. It was a glorious triumph for me and turned 2004 into a memorable and special year.

12 FINDING MY EDGE

'That intuitive, natural and intelligent driving instinct that was such a strength of Michael Schumacher and Ayrton Senna also, I believe, exists within myself'

MICHAEL SCHUMACHER, the brilliant seven-time Formula One World Champion, does not possess two heads and six arms – and neither do I. He is not some kind of super-human who is significantly different from the rest of mankind. Again, neither am I. Yet we have both found a way to win races and championships in motor racing, and to do so in successive seasons. People often ask me how I have done it, what the secret is. Well, I am not sure there is one. It is mostly down to dedication, desire and hard work. A bit of Guernsey grit helps, of course, but there are some things that need to be in place if you want to be a success in motor racing.

For a start, I would say it is particularly important to have really good reflexes; and I have been blessed with very good reactions. I like risky activities and sports, and have grown up keeping my reflexes razor-sharp that way. Most sports are good, particularly activities such as karting and motor cycling, and I test a lot in my day to day job, so that helps, too.

To stay sharp it's vital to look after yourself properly: to rest and prepare well, and not get too exhausted. It's also important to have a good nervous system – by that I mean one that helps you to stay calm and in control. By nature I am actually quite a nervous guy so, in one respect, I am quite amazed to be doing this job. As a child I used to worry terribly about all kinds of things; I am still a worrier, but have learned to handle it better and channel those nerves into something positive.

I am extremely self-critical but in a positive way. I am also honest with myself, will admit my mistakes and know my weaknesses and try to turn them into strengths; certainly Michael Schumacher was like that, which is why, I think, Ferrari loved him so much. Schumacher would come into the garage and admit if he had made a mistake. He was not afraid to do that and I think that also is very important. I do not like it when drivers are always blaming someone else for things that go wrong. You have to take responsibility if you crash or if you are slow or if you make a silly error. We all do it so we must all be able to own up to it and face the reality. I try always to do that. It is something I am proud of in myself. It means the team are more likely to respect me and we work better. I generally do not throw my toys out of the pram and act like a three-time world champion *prima donna*. That is due to my background, work ethic and my enormous desire not to waste both time and the energy I will need in the racecar.

Like Schumacher I am absolutely relentless. I do not give in and, in a lot of ways, the tougher it gets the better I become – and in my racing that really does help me.

I react in a very positive way to pressure. One of my mind coaches once told me I have an amazing 'laser focus' which, he said, he had never experienced with anyone else before. I am able, he told me, to lock on to something and concentrate totally in a way that shuts out everything else. In any sport that gives you a huge advantage. After all, nobody wants to be worrying about their tax return when they are approaching Eau Rouge, the famous zig-zag bends at Spa-Francorchamps, at high speed in teeming rain and poor visibility.

Another thing I save for racing is my energy, as I've already touched on. I like to hit a race weekend with a real excess of energy that I can draw on whenever I need to. So I make a conscious effort to conserve my energy when I am not racing. Indeed, sometimes, I will not talk for a long time nor concentrate on things unnecessarily. That's just my way of preparing myself properly.

However, my biggest personal strength is that I am very spiritual. I believe I can find a way of tapping into the universe, or a higher intelligence as I call it, that seems to offer such a wealth of experience and information.

I try to tap into that spiritual side of things. I think Ayrton Senna, the late, great, three-time World Champion, was inclined that way, as were the legendary British drivers Sir Stirling Moss and Sir Jackie Stewart. Each of them would look at the crowd and notice which way they were pointing and looking as he went round a corner; if the crowd was looking away they realised there had been an incident and acted accordingly.

That intuitive, natural and intelligent driving instinct that was such a strength of Michael Schumacher and Ayrton Senna also, I believe, exists within myself. At crunch times I am able to tap into that 'child' inside me and just trust myself to race naturally.

I have not only won four international touring car championships, I have won pretty much against the odds in series playing to rules designed to slow down the faster drivers. The championships always tended to go down to the final meeting of the season and I have been able to pounce at the crucial time. I am not perfect and have made mistakes in my career – turning down a Formula Vauxhall Lotus drive with the crack Paul Stewart Racing team and missing out on £60,000 was perhaps one – but

I believe my working methods, together with my spiritual side, certainly helped me succeed. And I hope my story can somehow inspire others, even if they don't have much money, to succeed in motorsport.

Another of my strengths is my ability to persuade people to help and sponsor me. I like to think that is because I try to give as much as I get. And not only to people in racing. I love my family and friends deeply, and am very protective of them and their feelings all the time. In return, that has helped me at crucial times in my career because I have felt they were living every lap with me.

That said, I have found that people do not always warm to me immediately. There is a coldness about me sometimes that I am aware of but which is just a form of shyness. I do not let people into my world very quickly. Although not intentional, maybe that is because I have become well known in Guernsey and that has made me a little protective of myself, my privacy and my home. While I try to be warm to as many people as possible it can often be quite mentally exhausting to do so.

My mentor Chris Cramer, the former British Hillclimb Champion, has given me some wonderful inspirational thoughts and moments of support in my life. He was the first man to tell me that motor racing is about 100 per cent commitment and 100 per cent restraint. He also used to say: 'The bullsh*t stops when the red light goes out.' Too true.

Thinking about the hype that surrounds racing, especially in Formula One, I admit I am a great fan of Briton Lewis Hamilton although I am concerned at the amount of media and public attention he receives all the time. There is too much hype and too many stories surrounding him, and it must be a distraction. I look at 2007 World Champion Kimi Raikkonen, on the other hand, and I think he has it all perfectly balanced.

The Finn is a finely honed racing tool. I'm told he says no to the £50,000 appearances, keeps a low profile, gives the media nothing ... and wins the championship. That is how I have been throughout my career, and although this single-minded approach probably has not helped me in some respects, it has certainly enabled me to win when it matters. Will I regret having been like that at the end of my career? We will see. But, for me, it has only ever been about the racing, my performances and the results.

I have always surprised people, I think. When I had my run in a Formula One car, as a prize, I thought it would be a single run just for fun. But it went so well that it turned into a test that was followed by more runs and tests. It was much the same when I was given a Formula Three drive with Renault: 'We'll give him a run, but it's only a prize ...' But as history shows, I managed to turn it into a full-time drive. At BMW, in touring cars, it was: 'We'll give him a chance, a one-year contract ...' And that single-year deal turned into three World Championship crowns and one European title.

Yet, for me, my career has not always stacked up in terms of results and recognition. Some drivers have actually gained greater recognition with fewer results. I have wondered sometimes if it's all down to hype and profile. Jo and I realised that nearly all of my championship-winning seasons had been highly competitive and therefore very satisfying but without much in the way of major television coverage. In Spiders, for example, when Jason Plato won the title two years before me, he not only enjoyed good television coverage but his prize was a very good road car and £30,000. I won the same championship in 1999, and won every single race, but did not get anything for it, as it went to the team to make up for the shortfall in sponsorship. It was the same with the British Hillclimb Championship. In the year that I won it there was no television coverage but there had been the previous year. The World Touring Car Championship is televised on Eurosport but not followed that closely in the United Kingdom; it is certainly a bigger series, in terms of coverage and audience, in Europe.

Thinking about it, I wonder sometimes if my relative lack of recognition, despite my success, is due to the shyness I have spoken about. Perhaps, as a three-time world champion, I should say to myself: 'Come on, Andy, go out there and do a bit more talking' for the sake of marketing the series. But I do not feel that is my job or that I would find it an easy thing to do. I very much want to see the series gain greater recognition, and would be happy if the same happens for me, but I would prefer to do that promotion via my racing.

I like to be the underdog, the chaser, the guy with the battle on his hands. It suits me. I grew up idolising Nigel Mansell – I think of his storming drives from the back of the grid and of when he almost fainted in the raging heat of Dallas to push his Lotus across the finish-line in the 1984 United States Grand Prix. I based a lot of my early days on Mansell's type of dogged determination. Even when I was last in my very first race I still believed I could win it. I believed that if I was relentless and determined, and never gave in, I would succeed. And I still fight for everything now, even when my car is not as fast as someone else's and I am fighting for position. Call it grit, determination or fight – I always use it.

So to anyone who wants to succeed in motorsport I tell them it is possible but they must keep working hard and believing. Without belief and grit it is almost impossible. And I know there are not too many drivers nowadays who will attempt to be successful without the right structure in place. Few come from humble, poor backgrounds. Maybe you could argue that Lewis Hamilton has come from nowhere, but he was in karting from an early age and enjoyed long-term support from McLaren chief Ron Dennis long before he made it to Formula One.

From the outside, I think Lewis always had the right momentum and his dad, Anthony, did a brilliant job looking after him, protecting him and guiding him. As for me, I cannot think of another driver who has gone from a small island with a 35 mph speed limit and no real racing pedigree to where I am now. I may be the only one.

I am sure there are great 'superstar' drivers all over the world, from poor families somewhere in China, Africa or Latin America, just waiting to be discovered, and I would love to help find them. It would be wonderful to discover a kid with loads of talent, and help him fulfil that and go all the way.

These days I am an experienced driver but still learning. I have found my style and know what works for me. It still revolves around a lot of hard work, believe it or not. Take overtaking, for example. When I can see somebody just ahead of me I get my head down and try to reel them in – and, in that situation, find I drive better and make fewer mistakes. It is the same whenever I am being followed by another car.

I work very hard outside the car, too. I am actually quite studious, make a lot of notes and am meticulous in my preparation. I think the more properly you can prepare, the more 'natural' you can be in the car. I guess this pretty much sums up my overall approach to racing. I am the same as anyone else, including Michael Schumacher. We are all given specific talents and it's up to ourselves to work hard to make the best of them. And there is nobody else to blame when things go wrong …

13 MACAU: BEATING THE ODDS

… 'Andy has now won the highest FIA Touring Car Championship four times in succession. This underlines his position as the most successful touring car driver of all time.'

I LOOKED OUT OF MY WINDOW on the approach to Hong Kong, leaning across the seat to watch the ocean and the land loom up and greet us. It was November 2005. I was about to arrive at a destination I had been dreaming about since my childhood: I was going to race to win a world championship.

I felt that I was ready for anything. I could see the sun sparkling on the water and the famous high-rise buildings reflecting the shimmering light beyond and between them. And I could see the wings of our Boeing 747 stretched out as we came in to land.

The South China Sea was covered in a patchwork of small boats of all shapes and sizes … and, as far as I could see, all ages. It was a long way from Guernsey, but the sight of the sea and all those amazing vessels floating around on the eastern side of the Pearl River delta offered a kind of familiar comfort to me.

No, it did not look at all like sleepy old St Peter Port on a sunny autumnal morning. But I was getting the right kind of buzz.

I have always enjoyed travelling. It must have something to do with coming from an island and growing up in boats and cars, and on bikes and so on. Like most Guernsey folk I am pretty self-reliant and resourceful.

I am not afraid of new experiences, and like to prepare properly and enjoy my travel. And going to Macau I knew what to expect. I had been before and was ready for the warm and sometimes hot weather and the slight humidity in the air together with the busy streets and bright, exciting atmosphere.

It was late autumn at home, with cold winds and rain, but I was flying into Hong Kong, the old British outpost that is one of just two 'special administrative regions' in modern China. I would take the ferry across the delta to the other, Macau, a former Portuguese colony with a long and equally colourful history as a trading post.

Unlike most people on my plane, I was not travelling as a tourist or to set up some lucrative business deals. I was there to race and become a world champion. I was tuned in like never before. I was determined to fulfil at least a part of my lifelong dream: to become Britain's first world motor racing champion in nine years following Damon Hill's lifting of the Formula One title for Williams in 1996. I was aiming to complete my debut season in the inaugural FIA World Touring Car Championship with BMW by taking the ultimate prize.

I had grown up a lot since that far-off day I left Guernsey in 1997. In those years of tough times I had gained experience and learned about the world – the rarefied world of motor racing and the real world of survival. I knew what it was like to have little or no money at all and to struggle for every penny.

I had also got married. Jo had moved over to Silverstone and we had lived in the caravan. I had cold-called everyone for sponsorship while, at the same time, having to rebuild my racing career because I did not know enough about single-seater racing. Then I had started to find my way.

None of it had been easy for us; keeping my family convinced it was all going to work out had certainly not been. All those tough times, including the work I had put in to move on from that caravan parked at Silverstone to progress through all those different race series – the Formula Renault winter series, Formula Three, Formula Palmer Audi, the Renault Spider Cup, the British Touring Car Championship and the European Touring Car Championship – floated across my mind like the boats on the sea.

I had proved my talent and speed, but in our business that is not always enough. Some people turn up with budgets bigger than anyone else's and then, when the decisions for race-seats are made, talent and potential is often a secondary consideration. Many times I had faced setbacks, some of them very serious, and had asked myself if I would be crazy to carry on. Jo, my rock, never lost her belief, though.

In the end, I found my niche when I signed to race for BMW Team UK and won a few races in the 2003 European touring car series. By any standards I had done well in some of the series I contested and, in fact, dominated a few, but they had not been lucrative for me in terms of earning big cash. In fact, it had been the other way round. I had been working flat-out to find the money to race the cars and win races.

But by the time I was on that plane to Macau in 2005, I was a man on a mission – and that, for me, meant winning races for my team in the FIA World Touring Car Championship. And this event, on the closed streets of the densely populated Macau peninsula, would decide who won the title. In every way, it was the end of the beginning for me but not, I hoped, the beginning of the end. I wanted to win it and go on winning.

* * *

To motor racing fans all over the world, Macau is something special. It is Asia's version of the Monaco Grand Prix, a classic street-circuit race set by the sea. And the Macau Grand Prix, for Formula Three cars, is a blue riband event at that level. The roads are lined with barriers and there's no room for error anywhere. It is one of racing's toughest tests. I had raced on those unforgiving steel-lined roads before and knew how tough it would be. So I had prepared myself well and ensured I was ready and in the right frame of mind. At the previous round of the World Touring Car Championship, at Valencia in Spain, I failed to win. Even so, I'd had a strong weekend. I may have only qualified in fifteenth place on the grid, but the BMW 320i was in far better shape for the warm-up and I managed to finish the first race in fourth position. All three title contenders were involved in a great fight for second spot in race two and I managed to finish on the podium. Fabrizio Giovanardi, in the factory Alfa Romeo, was second and Dirk Muller, in the BMW, fourth. Dirk and I had a few words afterwards!

So I had done enough to make sure that I went to Macau for the final two races of the season with a realistic chance of claiming the title. I was one point behind Muller, the championship leader, but that hardly mattered because there were three of us each with a good chance of becoming champion – myself, Dirk and Fabrizio.

The standard in that series was very high. So I knew I had to be at my best – and perhaps a bit more – if I were to beat them and win the championship.

The sport's ruling body, the Fédération Internationale de l'Automobile (FIA), had made sure the title race would be wide open by using a system of weight ballasts, reverse grids and various rule changes as the season progressed to maintain a level playing field. The harder you tried to win and pull away from your rivals, the tougher it became to succeed. Clearly the FIA did not want any one team, manufacturer or driver to dominate. So, here in China, the title scrap would be settled by small details and human errors, and the ability to stay clear-minded and focused, with the car in the right shape to do the job.

Although I knew Macau well I was not going to leave anything to chance – so I went out at two o'clock in the morning one day to take a close look at the track in a Mini Moke.

I had, of course, won a major title before. The previous season I had won the 2004 European Touring Car Championship for BMW in Dubai against the odds. I had prepared precisely for what would be a hot race that race weekend by training in my race suit with my helmet on – in a sauna. People thought I was crazy, but it worked. This time I did not need to do quite the same thing, only to make sure I stepped into the car with exactly the right mindset.

I was hungry and committed – that same feeling I had on the day I left Guernsey all those years before in 1997. My ambition might have changed a bit, but it was still alive. Okay, I was not in a Formula One car but this was still a race for my first world title.

I took six weeks off after Valencia. A camera crew followed me around, and that was a distraction and a bit of fun. My mind was busy but I needed to empty it so that by the time I got to Macau it would be easy to focus on the job.

As a racing driver you have to be ruthless like that and learn to see the things that you need to, and sometimes cut out everything else. To this end, I had been meditating for a while and knew it helped me.

The political stuff surrounding the championship was really cranking up as it came down to the 'business end' of the season. This would be the biggest meeting of my career, one spent largely fighting to reach a level where I felt I belonged and could prove myself. I wanted to win cleanly and fairly, and not be involved in anything else.

In my view, sport is all about the contestants involved giving their very best – and more if they can – and then seeing who wins. There is no place in top-level sport for anything other than fair, honest and true sporting competition, and I am sure most sportsmen feel the same. But, at the very top level of any sport, there are always certain other factors that can affect results.

For Macau, I was forced to carry the maximum amount of ballast on the car – 70 kg. That was a huge disadvantage and like carrying another adult in the passenger seat.

The ballast would definitely affect the car's balance, handling, tyres, just about everything. But I had put so much into my preparation that I was confident that, out there on the track, I would succeed. I had enjoyed a good test session during the six-week break and I was confident. I felt as if I was the man to beat.

On reflection, it was a bit of a miracle to even be in Macau and in with a chance at all. Yes, I may have won the European Touring Car Championship the year before, but the 2005 season – the first of the modern-day World Touring Car Championship – started pretty badly for me. The BMW 320i was very lively and I was not entirely comfortable with it. Yet, being a perverse kind of person and with my team's excellent engineering, I just carried on with it for the whole season even though it never suited my style. It was not my kind of car; it was very nervous on the real axle. Sometimes in this business, however, that can happen with a chassis. It's all part of the job.

Having said that, and even if I say so myself, I drove really well during the season. Somehow, I managed to pick up quite a few podiums during the early part of the campaign – and what a bonus they were to me when the going got really tough. Having won the European title the year before, a few people would have preferred it had I kept out of their way, slowed down or just not really competed … The World Championship meant a lot to all the manufacturers and they wanted to see their cars win, and that was entirely understandable.

My problem was that BMW Team GB was not the official test team for the Munich manufacturer. That honour had always gone to Team Germany and, to make matters worse, ours was only a one-car outfit. That meant, as the only driver, I had nobody to compare with in the same garage and had to work through my own data. But I think the team and I did a great job and I am sure our efforts also helped everyone else raise their own game.

I think BMW were happy. The actual problem existed more at the circuit. At first, as far as I could see, the whole company was ecstatic at my success. I loved racing for BMW and things were going well. When I first started, the goal was to win a race in 2003. We won three! In the second year, we followed that up with five race wins and I took the 2004 European Championship. It was good.

Yet, despite my successes and progress, I felt something was not quite right for me. For some reason, I always seemed to start each year on the back foot. I do not know if it was because we did not have the testing or technology behind us, but it has always been a big fight for me to get my car to the same level of competitiveness as the others – even though we eventually tended to end up that little bit faster. It is like I am locked into my own private battle, but it is always a nice feeling to deliver a good performance.

It was like that in 2005, another year with a lot of hard work and progress. I was strong in the first half of the season, but didn't take any wins. I was competing as hard as I could and, in the end, it even seemed as if I could win the championship despite going through the whole year without a win.

With four races to go we decided to make a significant change to the car. We introduced a fresh chassis and, in effect, gave ourselves a new car just when we needed it. We went to Oschersleben, in Germany, with the 'new' car and I felt happy with it straightaway. It was a great feeling. After all those other positions – fifth, second, third, fourth, third, second, fifth and sixth – bang! I went out and I won the first race. It was such a breakthrough and I felt as if I had got back my speed. I was flying again.

So I was still in the mix as the championship headed off to Istanbul in Turkey, where I finished third and ninth, and then Valencia in Spain for the penultimate double-header, where I came home fourth and third. I kept my title hopes alive with those results and knew that with the car we had I could clinch it in Macau if I was absolutely on the money and did not make any mistakes at all.

Fortunately, I managed to qualify fastest to give myself the best chance of winning the championship. But I knew, even as I did, how difficult it was going to be – everybody was so fired up. Alfa had a big chance of taking the championship and turned up with a very quick package. And I was there with mine, which I felt had been much more competitive since Germany.

Even though I was going to start from pole position, I knew that, over a whole race distance, the extra 70 kg of ballast was going to knock the edge off the car thanks to the tyre degradation and brake wear that is heavy in Macau. It was obviously going to be very tough, but I knew I had done a good job putting the car on pole. So I was satisfied, but very aware of the tough challenge I faced. That kind of situation, with three drivers all believing they can win the title, creates immense pressure. It is the same for everybody and we all handle that kind of thing differently. I have learned to do it well, in my own way. My mind-management has won me my titles and helped me to handle the pressure at key moments.

The year before, in Dubai, I had been the underdog, but this time everyone was ready for me. Nobody was going to take any prisoners. If you made an error with these guys – many of them vastly experienced drivers, a lot with Formula One careers behind them – they would eat you and spit you out. I knew that. It takes a really strong mind to be able to perform in that environment and still not make any mistakes while, at the same time, thinking to yourself: 'Maybe it is not possible for me to win but I will take the best position I can and find a way to pick up points.' I balanced everything up in my mind and I knew I could get there.

I made a good start in the first race, but Augusto in the Alfa just catapulted off the start-line, probably because his car was 40 kg lighter than mine. In that instant I knew there was going to be very little chance for me to beat him. My championship scrap was not with him but I had to be mindful that he was Fabrizio Giovanardi's team-mate and, therefore, act pretty sensibly.

I stayed with him anyway and we had all sorts going on behind us as everyone tussled and battled. The crowd loved it. It was a real spectacle, as it nearly always is in the World Touring Car Championship. The racing is often close and very tough with plenty of contact.

And was I motivated! I knew that the last thing I wanted was to be sucked into the battles behind me.

I knew, too, that I needed to stay where I was and finish with good points, even if it was behind Augusto. That would leave me in a good position, I was sure of that.

Macau is one of those places where you have to respect the circuit. I had a conversation with BMW ace Jörg Muller about two days before raceday and it really showed the competition that existed between the British BMW team and Team Germany. Jörg was not in the mix to win the championship but *was* in a position to influence it.

And he said to me: 'I am here to support my team-mate Dirk Muller and I am brilliant around Macau. I want my team to win it.' Even though ours was a BMW team and racing under the same manufacturer badge, it had basically told me: 'You've got no chance, mate. Don't even get out of bed!' That was great for me, just what I needed to hear – and a little more fuel for the fire.

When the race started Jörg was back behind me as was Dirk who, despite being in with a title shot, had not qualified particularly well.

I was working to my plan of avoiding trouble, not being sucked into scraps and collecting good points even if I could not win. And what happens behind me? Who careers off into retirement? Jörg Muller.

He speared off and into a tyre wall and his accident triggered a multi-car pile-up behind him. Some of the other cars scraped through, but several were ruled out of the game straightaway. The race was stopped and controlled under a Safety Car before being restarted.

When it was, I followed Augusto and finished second. The reverse grid system put me back to seventh on the grid for race two but I knew I still had a very good chance to win the title. I had not thrown it away and that was what that first race had been all about: coping with the pressure, staying on the track ...

Dirk had endured a terrible first race. His BMW's half-shaft broke on the final lap and that put him out of the points in tenth position. Fabrizio had a crash, on the eighth lap, and damaged his car. All this left Dirk as my only title rival going in to the second race.

It was obviously going to be a race with even more pressure than the first. But the greatest pressure was on Dirk as the championship leader. He also drove for Team Germany and so a lot of expectation sat on his shoulders. I was just the underdog from Guernsey, the guy racing for the British team that normally only ran one car although we had drafted in a second car that weekend for Dutchman Duncan Huisman to help me out.

I remember saying to Jo: 'Whatever happens in this race you can't celebrate. If somebody goes off into a tyre wall you can't celebrate. It's not very good on television ... don't do it.' I was conscious of the corporate image of the team and the manufacturer's reputation. But I don't think Jo gave a hoot.

As we approached the grid for race two you could feel the whole place buzzing. People hung from everywhere: houses, balconies and doorways. The crowd looked big. It was hot. A lot rode on the result and we all knew that. At the start, Dirk seemed to outbrake himself and locked up. Then, on lap two, he just blew up under all the pressure, losing his car and spearing off into the tyre wall. He gamely soldiered on, refusing to concede defeat, but eventually limped out of the fray.

The cameras showed Dirk's BMW flying off and then panned into my garage and to Jo's face. And there she was, my beautiful, loyal wife, jumping up and down, waving her arms and screaming with joy! What had I told her? From that point I was World Champion. That race is one I shall never forget. I went out hard from the start to win and pushed right on the edge. And I was doing so, Bart Mampaey, the team owner, came on the radio and said: 'Andy, you are the World Champion. Andy, you have won the title.' All my rivals had fallen away and I had done it – providing, of course, that I did not fall off as well in the remaining laps …

I started to relax, promptly went a lot faster and eventually closed up behind Duncan, my one-off team-mate. Somehow he had ended up leading the race, helped by not carrying any success ballast, of course.

Frustratingly, my team ordered me: 'Stay in position.' And I was thinking: 'What? I'm going to be World Champion. I want to win this last race!' But there was the team again ... 'Stay in position, stay there ...'

The yellow flags were out, which meant no overtaking, so I had to follow him around and he won the race. I had claimed one victory that year but so had many other drivers because the competition was so fierce. You received success ballast as soon as you won a race and at the next meeting you were nowhere.

It was my first world crown and it was my second championship title in a row. I was so happy to be the World Champion but pretty miffed at not winning that race – it was mine to take but the team had told me to hang back. So I took the title and just concentrated on that. I knew I had done what I had dreamed of in winning a world title and that, in my mind, made me feel like the best touring car driver in the world. It was a great feeling and meant so much to me.

For the record, I had claimed one win, twelve podiums, one pole position and three fastest race laps.

It had been a very demanding end to the 2005 season and the Macau Guia street circuit had been an outrageous track on which to race a 300 horsepower car. But I had taken pole, by a full second, shown real pace and gone on to control the two races. I finished second in both but know I could have won the second race. So had the team and so had Duncan, I am sure. Jo had been almost delirious with joy at that championship triumph and I shared her delight. A great feeling. We had climbed our first mountain and put Guernsey on top of the world.

A year later, in 2006, we were back in Macau. As usual, there was a lot of build-up and I had a meeting with a local journalist who had written a very negative preview. In his piece he had written that I had never been any good round Macau, that I had always played back-up to the works BMW team and I was not competitive.

To me, he just did not know what he was writing about. If you had asked anyone in the paddock who was the best driver I think most would have said me. He was just trying to spin a story. That year was a big one for me because I had a chance to retain the championship title – and did so. Afterwards this journalist was the first guy I sought out and, to be fair to him, he said: 'There you go, I was totally wrong. You are the man.'

I was glad to hear that because that first championship win in 2005 had meant so much to Jo and I.

That was not all there was to 2005 for me. The world title win was the icing – a thick layer, I must say – on a very good cake. I also managed to win – at the first attempt –

the classic Nurburgring 24-Hours race for GTR and touring cars with Pedro Lamy, Boris Said and Duncan Huisman, driving a BMW M3 GTR. The 'old' Nurburgring is one of those tracks at which you have to concentrate fully, especially in an endurance race like that. It has what seems like a thousand corners – in fact it has 172, 84 right and 88 left – but you need to drive it in a racing car to understand what I mean! After that victory, the car was gracefully 'retired' to the BMW Museum in Munich.

It would be an understatement to say it was a busy year because I also acted as a test driver for the BMW Williams Formula One team. Indeed, in one mad week in May, I not only raced in the Nurburgring race but did two days' testing for Williams at Vallelunga in Italy and raced in the World Touring Car Championship at Silverstone where I managed to score two podium finishes. I think that workload said a lot for my versatility not to mention my talent.

I received a lot of good publicity from that week and I was spoken of as 'the Michael Schumacher of touring cars'. Of course, I was proud to be compared in any way to such a great racing driver, but that kind of label tends to prevent people from thinking much beyond tin-tops. Nothing is ever simple, is it?

At the end of the year, I was extremely proud to win the British Racing Drivers' Club's Gold Star, the BARC Gold

Medal and a collection of other accolades. These included the Guernsey Ambassador of the Year award, and the Channel Islands and BBC South West Sports Personality of the Year prizes. On top of that, the Guernsey Post Office issued a set of six stamps entitled 'Fast Track to a World Champion' to mark my world title success.

On the back of all that, how could I not feel proud and motivated for the future? Jo and I had come such a long way together and now we were there, at the top. But we knew we had to carry on climbing. Although I was the champion, I had won just one World Touring Car Championship race in 2005 and I wanted to improve on that, so that, along with defending my title, would be one of my main targets for 2006.

As in the previous year, the 2006 season was tough with lots more fiercely competitive racing. But I managed to achieve my chief objectives. I registered five race wins and took three pole positions with the BMW UK team that was now running the 320si model.

Probably the most important victory came in the traditional season-closer at Macau when the chips were down. As ever, the meeting was decisive with nine drivers going into the showdown with a chance of taking the title – but I was so determined to hang on to my crown I gave it my absolute best. Qualifying was extremely wet and that inevitably played havoc with some drivers' chances of taking a decent grid position.

My closest rivals for the crown were Augusto Farfus, again racing an Alfa Romeo, and BMW Team Germany driver Jörg Muller. Jörg and me were level on points going into the weekend, but Augusto was just one in front, so it was all to play for. As usual, I prepared as thoroughly as possible, and concentrated on being in the best possible physical and mental shape for that weekend.

For the opening race I qualified on pole position and simply ran away in front to secure what was a really important win. I did not care what was going on behind me but, for the record, I have to say that the incidents did not do me any harm. On the first lap, Dirk Muller had a coming-together with Farfus. The clash left Muller's BMW almost blocking the track and, in effect, it ended his particular interest in the title. Farfus recovered but could only finish fifth and that meant I was looking good as we went to the second race. Incidentally, Yvan Muller's third place finish for Seat in the first race was low enough to take him out of the title fight along with Peter Terting, who was eighth, and Gabriele Tarquini in eleventh.

I knew what I had to do in the decider; in essence, the most important thing was to finish in the points. I duly did so without too much fuss, taking a fifth place to beat Jörg Muller by a single point and secure back-to-back world titles.

If it was not as exciting, in the purest sense, as my first the year before, it was arguably more satisfying – it is certainly more difficult in any sport to keep winning championships than to rise to the top in the first place. Still, it was an emotional and tearful triumph and meant a lot to me, my team, family and friends.

People say that it is not the getting there that is the hardest thing, it is the staying there. Well, I faced that problem and I refused to yield and I did stay there. And, again, of course, it was in Macau; the place that keeps cropping up so significantly in my racing career and where I have enjoyed some of the greatest moments of my career.

That success attracted yet more attention from a wider audience and at the end of the year I was awarded the BRDC's Gregor Grant Trophy, one of British motorsport's top awards. I was delighted and it capped things perfectly for both Jo and I as we were now enjoying life in a way we had never before contemplated.

When the 2007 season came round, it developed with a similar kind of scenario to those in previous years. There was a lot of incident and intrigue as the season unfolded – subjects I have already touched on elsewhere – and this resulted in another very close fight that, once again, reached its crescendo in Macau.

This time, I was level on points with Yvan Muller, driving for Seat, as we went into the twenty-second and final race. I should really have sewn up the title earlier at the previous meeting at Monza, but I'd endured a near-disastrous weekend, which allowed Yvan to catch up. Four other drivers were also in with a chance – including Augusto again, this time in a Schnitzer BMW, and Briton James Thompson in an Alfa Romeo – so I knew it would be heavy pressure all the way through.

I did not do myself any favours when I qualified a lowly twelfth, but everything seemed to come my way in the actual races. In the first, Yvan Muller suffered a fuel-pump failure and Augusto clashed with Gabriele Tarquini while I managed to deliver what was required to finish eighth and take the advantage.

With the reverse grid system running down to eighth place, I took pole position in my BMW 320si for race two. At the start, Nicola Larini, in a Chevrolet, made a slow start with a slipping clutch and James Thompson came up from the second row to take second place behind me. James pushed as hard as he could to get by and I defended. We made contact here and there, but he did not have the ultimate pace to pass me. He needed to win in his Alfa with me failing to score if he was to take the championship and there was no way I was going to let that happen.

After defending hard, Thompson fell back and that meant I could press on and try to open a sensible lead ahead of Larini who eventually came home second. It was not easy and I had needed a decent slice of luck, but it all came together in the end and I was World Champion again – for the third successive time. I knew it had needed a special combination of circumstances for me to be champion for a third time and I must admit I couldn't believe it at first. It's also worth pointing out that I had now been in five successive final race deciders seeking to win a championship and, including the European success in 2004, I had won four of those in a row.

I ended up taking the title by 11 points from Yvan Muller and BMW also won the manufacturers' title after resisting a strong challenge from Seat. The support and motivation supplied by Jo, my children and all my family was again very important to me and I also appreciated the words afterwards of BMW motorsport chief Dr Mario Theissen who said: 'To win such a close championship three times in a row is an outstanding performance. If you include the European Championship title from 2004, Andy has now won the highest FIA Touring Car Championship four times in succession. This underlines his position as the most successful touring car driver of all time.'

I had won only three races that season – at Porto in Portugal, Brands Hatch and Macau – but that is a reflection on the competitiveness of the series as much as anything else. I took two poles but I am sure that, without the penalty ballast system, I would have done better. That said, I had achieved what I really had to – defend my championship.

When I got home to Guernsey, just as in the previous years, I faced an emotional reception again. I just cannot stress too often how important the support I get from home is to me. I received more recognition from the UK media as well and I was once again honoured by the BRDC when it presented me with a Gold Medal, a prize only rarely given to a driver and the first time to one still competing.

Damon Hill, the president of the BRDC, delivered a very kind, warm and, for me, satisfying speech. It was only the eighth time the medal had been awarded by the club and I was truly touched when I received it at the BRDC's annual lunch at the Savoy Hotel in December. I felt as if I had reached another level. I looked at the names of the former winners – Sir Stirling Moss, Bernie Ecclestone, Sir Frank Williams, Martin Brundle, Ken Tyrrell, Ron Dennis and Murray Walker – and, to me, they were all legends. Three titles and now this, I thought … it was time to look ahead and find a new challenge.

14 STAYING AT HOME

'The owner poured us a glass of something – it may have been port – and encouraged us to have a party. When I took the opportunity to introduce Dr Theissen, the owner said: "Oh! Dr Theissen. Are you Andy's doctor?"'

I WAS MAGNETISED BACK TO GUERNSEY in early 2004.

The very reasons I left – to get away from the insular attitude, the quietness and the lack of momentum – were the actual reasons I returned. At this point in my life, and my career, I wanted that peacefulness and that 'special' lifestyle that the island offered. Most people who leave Guernsey are perhaps a little frustrated, but once they have moved away they tend to realise the grass is definitely not greener elsewhere. That's how it was for me.

There is so much wealth in Guernsey, but it's not something that's thrust in your face unlike in, say, Monaco. There are not many glamorous people in Guernsey. A family that lives in a little house on the edge of a cliff might actually be multi-millionaires, but the fact would be largely hidden and you'd never know any different.

Having said that, it has been a source of annoyance and frustration that, with so much money swimming around Guernsey, I couldn't generate some decent sponsorship early in my career – indeed, with it I may have got to Formula One fairly easily. At the end of the day, though, Guernsey doesn't owe me anything. And I still love the place and its people.

I came back to Guernsey as my own person, having forged out a successful career thanks to my own efforts, and it is a source of great pride that I am now one of the most successful people on my home island. For years, I hankered after more publicity and more recognition so I could attract more sponsorship. But now I think the opposite.

Strangely, I have spent a lot of time over the last few years actually trying to lower my profile on the island, and it is a conflict within me that is not easy to reconcile. I like the recognition, of course, and it means a lot to me, and I love Guernsey so I want to give something back. But, at the same time, it is important to me that I can come home and enjoy a private life. If I appear too much in public I will be recognised and, however enjoyable it is to chat to my fellow islanders, it does tend to take up a great deal of energy and eats into my relaxation time if I am, for example, enjoying a day on the boat with my family.

If that's the downside, the positive is when a little old lady stops me and asks for a photo because she says she is my biggest fan. That is magic and really motivational.

There was a lot of fuss at one stage when media commentators were putting me forward for an MBE. I have never pushed to receive one, but it was suggested on the front page of the *Guernsey Press and Star*, the island's local newspaper. While I would loved to have received an MBE at that time, both for Guernsey and myself, I never wanted to be the cause of such stories.

As it happens, however, I was actually in line to receive an MBE for my successes in motor racing around the time this book was published. That is a great honour for me and my family, one I hope brings much pride to all my fantastic fans in Guernsey.

While I am relatively ill at ease with the public profile that comes with recognition and success, I do feel fairly comfortable working with the media as an extension of my job.

One thing I do believe is that a lot of islanders do not actually realise the level I have now reached in my career – that the World Touring Car Championship is a truly global series and, along with Formula One and World Rally, among the top three motor racing series on earth. This is, I think, a spin-off from the way that television operates and in which satellite stations, particularly Sky, have dominated sport so much in the last few years. The real motor racing fans, who read the specialist magazines and follow the sport closely, know all about me and my achievements, but the ordinary sports fan in the street – even if he lives in Guernsey and he has heard of me – does not really appreciate what the fuss is all about.

Not long ago, for example, a guy was at my house fitting some windows and a few days later he told his salesman about the jobs he had recently done. He mentioned my name and his colleague apparently exclaimed: 'What, Andy Priaulx? The World Champion?' The window fitter simply had not realised how well known I was. In fact, many islanders do not realise what motor racing is like at all and some still ask me why I do not race in the local hillclimbs any more …

I suppose that is actually a good thing because if everyone knew my background, I would surely have no peace and quiet at all. I am certain Lewis Hamilton, Michael Schumacher, Fernando Alonso, Kimi Raikkonen and all those Formula One guys who have gone to live in Switzerland appreciate its solitude and peace as much as they do any tax advantages.

There was another good reason I wanted to return to Guernsey when we did. In the six or so years we had been away I had gone from being 'Pikey Priaulx' living in a caravan to a married man with a family. Sebastian was by then growing up fast and Danniella arrived the year before while I was away, as always, in Macau. We were still living in Towcester, near Silverstone, but the pull to return home was strong for both Jo and I. When I signed for BMW, I put the wheels in motion to make the move back to my family and roots. I wanted it not just for personal reasons but because I wanted to be certain my family would be safe when I was working away.

In Guernsey, I do not have to worry about the house being broken into or the general stress and wear and tear of life in England. The downside, and what my team dislikes most, is that I am not in direct or easy access to mainland Europe. And it can be exacerbated by the island's airport having a tendency to get fogbound in winter.

Another interesting aspect of Guernsey is that it has very few shops. It's not a place where people delight in parting with their money. There is also no discernible fast-food culture. Guernsey is about the sea and the land, through which most people make their living, and the beaches where our kids can enjoy themselves. Guernsey is, in a way, an island that is frozen in time. It is an acquired taste and maybe not ideal for young people looking for excitement and big career opportunities.

A good example of how Guernsey folk are unaffected by fame or fortune happened when BMW motorsport chief Dr Mario Theissen and his wife Ulrike visited the island and my family for the first time. They told me they could not believe the beauty of the island as we went walking and did other things together. I actually felt quite a lot of pressure; I could not believe this high-profile guy would want to hang out with me for a week. I felt really honoured. But as well as being an extremely important guy in motorsport circles he is a very nice one – and I am not just saying that because he once said, so I'm told, that he thought I was the best driver in the world!

One day, we went to a lovely little restaurant called La Sablonerie in a tiny hotel in Sark. As Sark is an island where motor vehicles are banned, we took a horse and carriage for the final part of our journey having crossed the sea by boat. The owner poured us a glass of something – it may have been port – and encouraged us to have a party. When I took the opportunity to introduce Dr Theissen, the owner said: 'Oh! Dr Theissen. Are you Andy's doctor?'

It did not matter at all when I explained he was actually the head of BMW motorsport. She just treated him in exactly the same way. And Dr Theissen did not mind at all. He is a very humble man with a great sense of humour. It was just a typical Channel Islands scenario.

After our meal, Dr Theissen was first to leave and jumped back into the horse and carriage – and slammed the door. What he did not realise, and what I had forgotten to warn him, was that shutting the door was a sign for the horse to go.

So there we were left standing as he disappeared off down the road on a driverless horse and carriage. I was pretty concerned, as you can imagine. It was not the conventional way for someone like me to host one of the most important bosses in the company ...

To his credit, Dr Theissen found it all highly amusing and when we eventually headed off together he said he was disappointed with the horse's speed. So he slammed the door again and the horse shot forward once more! He loved it.

I wanted to make a good impression on Dr Theissen and his wife so I had borrowed a luxurious Sunseeker boat to take us home. It was supposed to be the perfect way of completing our outing, a comfortable ride across the sea and back to the island. But it did not quite work out that way ...

I do not think any of us were too impressed when we got caught in a Force 7 storm while making the crossing. Unfortunately, Jo felt sick, the tables were thrown upside down and we were all tossed around like you would not believe.

I looked at Dr Theissen standing drenched at the back of the boat and worriedly thought: 'Oh no, what next? I really have to get him home in one piece.'

He roared aloud: 'Andy, this is absolutely fantastic!' He felt fine. And he was revelling in the whole raw experience of the storm. The girls were crying, the boat was pitching and the rain was teeming down, but he was in heaven. I think it was an experience he enjoyed and remembered for a long time. It was also an experience that reminded me why I had decided to go home.

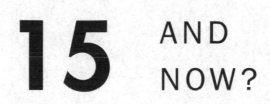

15 AND NOW?

'I am, I believe, the first man born in the Channel Islands to be crowned a motor racing world champion – and return to do work on road safety!'

OUR DAUGHTER, DANNIELLA, was born at the Princess Elizabeth Hospital in Guernsey at 2.17 am on 17 November 2003. She weighed just 2.9 kg and was five weeks premature. At the time, predictably enough, I was away, in Macau for the season-ending meeting in that year's European Touring Car Championship. Yet, far worse for me than those bare facts was the knowledge that Jo was very unwell at the time of the birth and her life was in danger. She was suffering from pre-eclampsia and at one stage the doctors thought all her body organs were in danger of shutting down.

There was nothing I could do.

I was staying at the Mandarin Hotel in Macau, waiting for my little daughter to be born many miles away and hoping my wife was going to be fine. I understood the dangers because we had been through it before but I was still very worried.

Seb, our son, had been born nearly three years earlier at Northampton General Hospital at 7.02 pm on 18 January 2001. He weighed only 1.78 kg and was also born prematurely – at 36 weeks. When Seb was born, the umbilical cord had wrapped around his neck and Jo had pre-eclampsia. Seb did not feed properly and both he and his mother were unwell for a long time. In fact, as he recovered, we had to feed Seb through his nose as he took just 1 ml of food per hour by tube.

At least then I was at home to help care for him when Seb, who was so tiny, was fighting for his life. In fact, we nearly lost Seb. One more day at the hospital and he would have died, we were told.

So when I was in Macau in 2003 and Jo rang to tell me she was going to hospital, I knew what might happen. 'I'm going in to have the baby, I'm going in Andy,' she said. I felt so helpless.

I remember looking out over the bridge in Macau. It was night-time, long after the racing had finished, and I had gone to bed. The phone rang. I didn't hear it but eventually they tried Tim Thomson next door, who stormed into my room and threw his mobile at me. 'Jo's having the baby … Wake up!' he shouted.

There was nothing I could do.

But I knew I could not sleep. I paced around wondering what was going to happen. Tim ordered everything on the room service menu but I ate nothing. Apparently, Jo's medical readouts were the worst the medical staff in Guernsey had ever seen and her body should have simply shut down.

Yet, somehow, the medics managed to deliver Danniella, who promptly went on to oxygen, and they saved Jo. Tim and I cried our hearts out in relief.

Because of that I always have memories of Macau. Not just the championship wins but other, more personal, recollections. Dannii's birthday always falls during the Macau weekend. So, one day, I am going to take her there to celebrate her birthday – and actually spend it with her.

When I arrived home after Dannii's birth, I spent the next month to six weeks getting Jo healthy again. Dannii was born prematurely but she was now okay. Jo, however, was struggling and had contracted hepatitis through food poisoning. It was one thing after another.

We had two pretty tough births – much tougher for Jo than for me, of course – but we pulled through and learned so much – particularly that life is precious. There are so many people who do wonderful work that most of us never even think about. These experiences not only showed me this but they also taught me to re-evaluate and make the best use I can of my own life.

Indeed, despite my racing successes, the thing of which I am most proud in my life is becoming a father to two beautiful kids, a husband to a gorgeous wife, and being able to feed my family and see them grow up. I have been able to buy my own house and be my own man.

My children gave me a special motivation to succeed. And I vowed to make a difference to others who faced similar circumstances to ours. That is another reason why I am glad to be living back home on the island.

Apart from my close interest in premature babies I love helping children. They give me a very special feeling and I especially like being involved with underprivileged kids who do not have the best opportunities in life. It gives me a real buzz at races to let them wear my crash helmet and have a good look over the car, and talk to them about their dreams.

Our experiences with the births of Seb and Dannii led to the creation of the Priaulx Premature Baby Foundation in 2001. We wanted to help other families who were going through the same ordeal as Jo and I had. We have used it to raise much-needed funds for the cause – to date, more than £50,000 – and provide some major donations to the Guernsey Premature Baby Unit. This has, for example, enabled the unit to buy a new brain monitor so as to prevent babies and their families having to travel to mainland Britain for care. Indeed, when we were told of the first occasion it had actually helped a baby and its parents in that way, we were delighted.

Jo and I are, in fact, both keen to support as many local charities as we can. Guernsey has been good to me and my family, and I am proud to do my bit.

When the Guernsey Post Office issued stamps in my honour in both 2006 and 2008 I felt very privileged. The second set, in early 2008, was described as being 'just a miniature set' and at first I was not sure – I thought it was referring to my height! But when they were unveiled at Stanley Gibbons, the famous stamp shop in London's The Strand, I knew the producers were serious. I have had a lot of my achievements lauded in my career, but to be commemorated in such a way, and with the approval of Her Majesty the Queen, is amazing. It makes everything you do, including all the community and charity work, seem even more worthwhile.

And I am very proud Her Majesty chose to honour me again in 2008 in her annual Birthday Honours by presenting me with an MBE. It is an honour that reflects not only on me but on Jo, my father, Graham, who has done so much to support my career, all my family, and the people and the island of Guernsey. As a Channel Islander, I know that the Bailiwick of Guernsey does not choose its heroes lightly so I am truly delighted to have been honoured by my home island. I certainly could not have achieved what

I have without my home support or the excellence of both BMW and my racing team RBM and Bart Mampaey.

There are many off-track activities I am involved in but one of the most important to me is road safety. We are very careful drivers in Guernsey, where the speed limit is 35 mph, but you can never take it for granted that the roads are safe as they can be.

This was brought home to me in 2007 when one of my friends, my mind coach Ian Pollock, was run over on the island. It was a terrible shock. I do not serve on any road safety committees, but since that accident I have started to help with various things in that area and I hope to do more of that in the future.

Indeed it seems almost ironic that I am, I believe, the first man born in the Channel Islands to be crowned a motor racing world champion – and return to do work on road safety!

For the moment, however, I have decided that you are a long time retired from motor racing and feel I have some good years left in me yet. I can still see myself racing in five years' time, but I certainly do not want to be one of those guys who stretches out his career for too long.

I also want to be young enough to achieve something positive in business, and to give something back to the sport, when I finish driving. That is why I set up Andy Priaulx Performance Management in February 2008. Experience is a key attribute in motorsport and now I have plenty of that I want to pass it on. There is very little independent advice available to anybody new to the sport who is serious about establishing a professional career. I know that from my own efforts. There are excellent programmes in place for established drivers, but not for those at a lower level. That is where I want to help.

In the long term I look at performance management and believe I can really help guide young drivers. The network of contacts I have built up over the last 15 years in motorsport has, and will, become invaluable. Some of the guys I have worked with over the years now work in top jobs in Formula One. I would love to find the next world champion – just so long as he does not come along and beat me!

I honestly feel that had I put the energy I have expended during my racing career into business I would have made a lot more money – although I would not have had the same amount of fun. I also do not think I would be the same guy now had I not experienced all those failures, and had to pick myself up over and again. One thing true about motor racing is that you do get instant feedback, and your results will decline the moment you are not 100 per cent focused; in business a lack of focus might not become apparent for a year or so. The saying goes that racing drivers do not make good businessmen, but I *had* to become a good businessman to become a racing driver. I think I have disproved that particular saying.

I would also like to explore a little bit within motor racing. Indeed, one ambition I do have is to win the classic Le Mans 24 Hours sportscar race one day. I am very lucky to have various people phone up and present me with opportunities and deals I could have only dreamed of ten years ago. Then, it was about finding enough money to survive the next month. Now, with money in the bank, it is about me picking and choosing what I want to do.

I am not saying I am now wealthy enough to kick back and retire, but money is now just part of the decision process rather than the be-all and end-all. When I decide which team to drive for, I now look at which gives me the best chance to win before I look at financial packages, which is a great position to be in. Derek Warwick was responsible for giving me my first chance in touring cars, and has always been a friend and supporter. It is to people like Derek and my dad, as well as a host of others that I must send my thanks – without them I would not be in this luxurious position now of pondering what to do with my future.

David Grace, a director of Scottish & Newcastle brewery, is another to whom I owe a lot. When I think of David I recall the time when I was trying to secure my Renault Formula Three contract and I recall novelist Paulo Coelho once saying: 'When you truly want something, the whole of the universe conspires to help you.' David was a friend of mine from hillclimbing and invited Jo and I for Sunday lunch one weekend. At the time I had no idea how I was going to pay the first instalment of my Renault deal. It was a crunch time in my career.

David pulled me aside and told me: 'If you need to make something happen, just let me know.' It was a Sunday lunch that turned into a monumental day for me because David stumped up the cash to keep me racing.

When I look back at my career I think if that particular meeting had not happened I would never have made it. There were a few other times like that: getting the BRDC sponsorship for Formula Three, Jo's friends finding some money to keep me going, Pete Berry's company bailing me out with £50,000 when I needed it badly, and Gary and Pam Dearn, a couple who were very close to Jo and I in England, also helping. And when Tim Thomson bought me a Renault Spider to race it was another of those make-or-break moments. None of what followed in my career would have happened without these people.

I have always tried to put out all the right messages without actually asking people for help. At times if you focus on getting money it just comes to you and at other times if you focus on the bills all you get are bills. There are dozens of people I am grateful to but I am glad that I believed in the Coelho credo!

My time with BMW has allowed me to become an international racing driver, to use the best equipment and to drive a Formula One car. Going from being a clubby grassroots racing driver to testing a Grand Prix racecar is something really special. I am certainly proud of my achievements with BMW.

I have chased a dream in a difficult and competitive environment, one that has an unbelievably high failure rate. So many of my former team-mates have failed to make it in the sport and so to have weathered all those storms and made it through gives me a great sense of pride.

I race for BMW, one of the best manufacturers in the world, and winning titles has earned me a great deal of respect. To be seen by those working at the highest level of the sport as someone whom they would like to speak to and take advice from is a special kind of recognition. The BRDC Gold Medal has been awarded to very few people – I felt privileged to receive it in 2007 and was so proud when Damon Hill, the president of the BRDC, read out the citation.

I would never claim to be the greatest or to belong at the very highest level, but I am proud to have achieved successes and thankful to the inspiration of my heroes. Nigel Mansell, Ayrton Senna and Lance Armstrong, the cyclist, are three of a kind in having their dedication and intensity carry them such a long way.

My toughest rivals have been the guys I have fought wheel to wheel with over the years: Gabriele Tarquini, Jörg Muller, Dirk Muller, Augusto Farfus and James Thompson. But, in this business, heroes and rivals are often intermingled because we all race together. I remember how I felt at the Race of Champions at Wembley in 2007. It was fantastic. I made the semi-finals and was one race away from facing Michael Schumacher, the seven-time World Champion, which would have been unforgettable. He is a guy who respected me and wanted to talk to me – and that's one of the biggest honours I have ever had.

Alex Zanardi, the Italian former Champ Car champion and now a touring car driver, is another guy I have huge respect for. He had his legs amputated following a racing accident but he likes a laugh and jokes about himself. He is such a straightforward, lovely guy. Whenever you are having a bad day, and you see him falling over and laughing about his own difficulties with a big smile on his face – and I can tell you it happens pretty often – it brings a tear to your eye. For me, he is so inspirational. We park our motorhomes together at race weekends and I think we are very similar. We are both emotional people and I was the first driver to hug him when he won his first race after his accident at Oschersleben in 2005.

I do not know if Alex and the other guys exactly share my views on our sport, but I have to say I am not a fan of 'success ballast'. It seems to me that the rule is always going to be open to some kind of manipulation but, that aside, the biggest problem I think is that race fans do not understand it. If you want new people to enjoy our sport they will be turned off by such complicated rules; in fact, we do not even display the amount of ballast we are carrying on our cars anymore.

I received an awful letter once that claimed I always had to rely on the reverse grid system to win touring car races. People simply did not understand that I may have had the heaviest car that weekend and that I had only just scraped into the top eight despite having driven my heart out. Actually I have done some research on my results and it showed that I was one of the least likely to benefit from the reverse grid system and win races.

I am not a fan of the ballast because you spend your whole career trying to get yourself into the best situation, and with the best manufacturer, to show your speed and win races. When you finally manage to manoeuvre yourself into the optimum situation ... the officials slow you down and stop you from winning.

I understand why they do it, however. There is probably less chance of manufacturers being involved without the ballast rule being in place. But that is such a shame: it is like backing a horse just before it crosses the finish line. Manufacturers will only put their money in if they think they are going to win. Is that sport?

I am a racer and the idea of ballast goes against that ideal. It is like telling a 100 metres runner to strap lead weights to his ankles because he ran too quickly in the last race. It is all about the crowd wanting to see a new winner. Sometimes I have had very important sponsors who I have wanted to impress at a race and performed better than anyone else yet finished down the field.

Last year in Mexico I drove one of the best races of my life and finished eighth. It probably looks meaningless in the record books, but I know that I earned one single point for BMW – and that was perhaps the hardest-won point of my career.

By the end of the season the guys leading the championship are normally fighting it out for a few points here and there rather than for wins. In 2006, nine drivers could have won the title on the last day! You might as well just turn up for one race and not bother with the rest of the season …

I have heard people say it is time for a manufacturer other than BMW to win. At the start of 2008 an engineer came up to me and said: 'Good luck, but I hope somebody else wins. I would like to see a new winner.' I thought that was awful. I realise that some people may find it boring when the same person wins all the time, but personally I think people should be admired for dominating.

I have enormous respect for Schumacher, Rossi, Armstrong, golfer Tiger Woods and tennis player Roger Federer for doing exactly that. I was once told that to win a race is really, really difficult and to win a championship almost impossible. I have won impossible championship after impossible championship and I think people should admire that.

But the truth is they do not. They just get bored. And they are encouraged to expect something else. Schumacher won seven world titles but had to sweat for every one of them. He had to work hard at his driving, leave his family behind for the majority of the time and risk his life. Sometimes you become more famous for being a runner-up, for being an underdog, simply because people feel sorry for you.

If you stand out in the crowd you tend to get more flak. When you win a championship you have a lot of extra responsibility and it makes it much harder to repeat that success. I know, I have been there and done it. And yet I want to do it again.

The World Touring Car Championship is one of only three major world motor racing series and it is well respected, as I have learned from talking to Formula One drivers and World Rally Championship guys.

That said, I admire the marketing of the British Touring Car Championship. In many ways I would enjoy a higher profile in the UK if I drove in that series, but it is not like it was ten years ago with major manufacturers putting in big money to win it. From a driving point of view I think the World Touring Car Championship is where all drivers want to be. But the British Touring Car Championship may yet be a part of my future.

Formula One is still the pinnacle of the sport. I admire it and everybody involved in it. It is so hi-tech and has some of the best drivers in the world. Not all of them, though. I like to think that if you took some of the best drivers out of World Touring Cars and put them in Formula One they would be competitive. I also believe if you took some of the best out of Formula One and put them in my series they would not necessarily win races straightaway.

I also love the nation versus nation concept of A1GP. I have been lucky to be invited to commentate for Sky on television at some of the A1GP races and it has been a refreshing experience. The series taps into a new audience and the racing has been fantastic, but I think it will always be a feeder series into Formula One and nothing will ever challenge that.

Looking across a wider landscape, I think NASCAR in the US is a marketing phenomenon and I would love to spend a year or two racing in the United States. But first I might have to try and convince BMW to build NASCAR engines ... And then there is Le Mans, as I've mentioned. I had hoped to race in this year's 24 Hours for Peugeot but there was a clash of dates. It was a big disappointment because that is something I very much want to do.

Maybe if I won an event like that it would boost my profile in Britain. It is unusual that my profile is much higher in mainland Europe than at home. I once walked into a restaurant in Spain and was not only recognised but given a standing ovation. Now that would never happen in Britain.

I am far more likely to be stopped for an autograph at Munich airport than at Gatwick or Heathrow. I know I am marketable, but in the UK I have paid a price for World Touring Cars being shown only on the Eurosport television network that is watched much more widely in Europe. In the UK, the British touring cars drivers are more widely known because their competition is shown on national television.

In the end, the most important thing to me is that I have recognition in my sport. Wherever I go, anywhere in the world, I now have respect for what I have achieved. When I visited the 2008 Spanish Grand Prix at Barcelona, I was treated with great respect by everyone in the paddock and that made me really happy. It proved that people do follow the World Touring Car Championship and those who are seriously involved in motorsport do respect my results. It proved to me that being a three-time world champion is an achievement that is noticed and admired.

For a guy who left Guernsey with just hope and a caravan that's something to be proud of. So while I am enjoying the racing and have the motivation to go on, I aim to carry on trying to win a few more titles.

ANDY PRIAULX
CAREER

Born: 8 August 1973, Princess Elizabeth Hospital, Guernsey.
Family: Parents Graham and Judy, sister Fiona, wife Jo and
children Seb and Dannii.
Career: Race winner in touring cars, single seaters, endurance
racing, hill climbing, karting, motocross and power boating.

Career Highlights:
2007
FIA World Touring Car Champion (BMW Team UK) with 3 wins,
2 pole positions
BRDC Gold Medal

2006
FIA World Touring Car Champion (BMW Team UK) with 5 wins,
3 pole positions
BRDC Gregor Grant Trophy

2005

FIA World Touring Car Champion (BMW Team UK) with 1 win,
    12 podiums, 1 pole position, 3 fastest laps
Nürburgring 24hrs Winner in BMW M3 GTR with Pedro Lamy, Boris
    Said and Duncan Huisman
F1 Official test driver for BMW Williams F1 Team
BRDC Gold Star
BARC Gold medal
Guernsey Ambassador of the Year
Channel Island Sports Personality of the Year
BBC SW Sports Personality of the Year

2004

FIA European Touring Car Champion (BMW Team GB) with 5 wins,
    9 podiums, 1 pole position, 6 fastest laps
Macau BMW Team Germany/Schnitzer Motorsport. Qualified 2nd,
    1st leg finished 2nd, 2nd leg finished 2nd
Autosport British Competition Driver of the Year
Channel Island Sports Personality of the Year
BBC SW Sports Personality of the Year

2003

European Touring Car Championship. 3rd overall (BMW Team GB)
    with 3 wins, 8 podiums, 1 pole position, 1 fastest lap
Macau BMW Motorsport/Carley Motors. Qualified 4th, 1st leg
    finished 2nd after leading for half of race, 2nd leg DNF
Australia HRT Holden Kmart Racing
Sandown 500, finished 12th
Bathurst 1000, did not start due to start line accident
BMW Sports Trophy for non-works BMW drivers

2002
Australia HRT Holden Kmart Racing. Team mate Yvan Muller
Queensland 500 and Bathurst 1000 6hr endurance races
BTCC Honda Racing UK. 5th overall with 1 win, 2 podiums, 2 pole
    positions

2001
Intl. F3: Qualified on pole and finished 2nd in Korean Super Prix
    beating 6 current F3 champions. Top British driver in Macau
    GP at 6th overall
BTCC EGG BTCC Team (invitation drive). 2 races, 2 pole positions,
    1 podium
British F3: Alan Docking Racing. 6th overall with 2 race wins,
    10 podiums, 2 pole positions
Nissan Open Telefonica (invitation drive). Finished 5th and
    challenged for 3rd in race 2

2000
British F3 Team Renault UK. Replacing Jenson Button. 3 podiums,
    1 pole position
Intl. F3: Manor Motorsport. Macau GP, 9th and 8th in races.
    Korean GP, top British driver in qualifying, DNF in race

1999
Renault Spiders: Team Mardi Gras. Champion with 13 wins,
    13 poles, 11 fastest laps in 13 races. Most successful
    Renault Spider driver of all time
BTCC Test drives for Renault, Vauxhall and Ford
Autosport/BRDC Club Driver of the Year
BARC President's Cup for Outstanding Achievement
Guernsey Ambassador of the Year

1998
Formula Palmer Audi Winter series. 2nd overall with 3 2nd places,
    1 3rd place, 1 5th place, 1 pole position
Renault Spiders Team Mardi Gras (part season). 2 lap records,
    1 pole position, 2 2nd places. Renault Spider Cup was
    forerunner to current Renault Clio Championship
Offered Nissan touring car test

1997
British F3 Speedsport/TOMS GB

1996
Formula Renault Startline Racing (part season)

1995
British F1 Hillclimbing RAC/MSA British Champion with 10 wins,
    8 lap records in 10 events
Nominated for BRDC Driver of the Year
HSA Driver of the Year
Offered drive with Paul Stewart Racing

1993–94
British hillclimbing Driver of the Year, 2 wins

1991–92
Clubmans hillclimbing Channel Islands champion, 2 lap records

1990
250cc Motocross Channel Islands champion, 2 lap records

1986
Karting: Consistent front runner

INDEX